For Michael Eisner

The Evans Guide for

COUNSELING DOG OWNERS

To the Monks of New Skete

The Evans Guide for
COUNSELING DOG OWNERS

by Job Michael Evans

With Illustrations by
Carol Lea Benjamin

Foreword by Michael W. Fox,
D. Sc.; Ph. D.; B. Vet. Med;
MRCVS

First Edition—Second Printing
1985

HOWELL BOOK HOUSE INC.
230 Park Avenue
New York, N.Y. 10169

Library of Congress Cataloging in Publication Data

Evans, Job Michael.
The Evans guide for counseling dog owners

Includes index.
1. Dogs—Training. 2. Pet owners—Psychology.
I. Title.
SF431.E93   1984   636.7′08′87   84-19324
ISBN 0-87605-660-5

Some of the material in this book appeared in *Off-Lead—The National Dog Training* monthly, and in *Animals* in slightly different form.

All illustrations copyright by the artist, Carol Lea Benjamin. Some of them appeared in *Pure-Bred Dogs/American Kennel Gazette.*

Excerpts from *No Way to Say Goodbye* appeared in the March, 1983, *Pure-Bred Dogs—American Kennel Gazette.*

Manufactured in U.S.A.

Contents

Foreword

I RECENTLY RECEIVED a telephone call from a gun-dog trainer and hunter who had just gone to a gun-dog trial and he was in a state of shock and outrage. Several competitors' dogs seemed to behave like zombies, and the man discovered that they had been trained with remote control shock collars. He was in his seventies and this was his last trial, not because of his age, but because of what humans have done to animals in the name of progress. He had had enough of this Brave New World, with its impersonal, high-tech controls and lack of traditional common sense morality, ethics and empathy. The shock-trained dogs were like mindless robots, simply working for and not with their "masters," like well-oiled machines.

This machine-world view is called Cartesianism after the 17th century French philosopher Rene Descartes. He proposed that animals are unfeeling machines, mere automatons, echoing physicist Newton's view of the universe as a complex mechanical system. These philosophical and scientific "advances" formed the post-Copernican world view of industrial society. Some religious strains of thought gave divine authority to this world view by declaring that animals do not have souls like we have, and that Nature has no inherent divinity. An omnipresent, inhering divinity in all things was regarded as "pagan" and pantheistic, though many noted non-mechanistic scientists today, such as Albert Einstein and Konrad Lorenz, hold firmly to pantheism, which is Albert Schweitzer's theosophical basis for a reverence for all life. This spiritual attitude toward all life stands in opposition to the materialistic and mechanistic one of our industrial civilization. By "un-souling" animals and desecrating Nature, we are absolved from any responsibility (and guilt) toward those of God's creation whom we exploit. A mechanistic and materialistic attitude toward animals and Nature has evolved such that the way in which we perceive, think, and relate to other living things, and the way in which we structure reality, is based upon power and control. The consequences of this world view are highly destructive of the natural world, and as animals and people alike are objectified, they are "deanimalized" and dehumanized—like today's "clockwork" dogs with electro-shock collars, and the obedient proletariat in *Clockwork Orange* and George Orwell's *1984*.

Dogs are not little machines governed by automatic, unconscious drives and instincts. They, like us, have interests, needs, wants, emotions; and they can reason and think, empathize and demonstrate altruism, qualities that many believe to be exclusively human, and misguided and anthropomorphic if applied to animals. Such is the ignorance and insensitivity of this arrogant, human-centered world view!

We are learning that we cannot live by power alone. While science has helped us understand the mechanisms of life, there is a subjective, emotional and spiritual dimension to reality that we must also understand, respect and empathize with. The old world view is responsible for the social, medical and environmental nemesis that we are experiencing today. It is being challenged and transformed by a more holistic and empathetic world view, which this book by Job Michael Evans embraces.

This is, therefore, a "New Age" book that takes us beyond the mechanistic view of dog-as-machine-to-be-trained. Through his counseling approach, the author provides the key to developing a wholly new, holistic perspective and a more empathetic and effective approach to dog training and behavior problems. We do not need power and control when we have love and understanding, be it in our relationships with each other, with animals, or with Nature.

—MICHAEL W. FOX, D.Sc., Ph.D., B.Vet. Med., MRCVS,
Scientific Director, The Humane Society of the United States

Introduction

LOVE IS the perfect beginning, the inspiration for taking on the responsibility of owning a dog. And it's the only possible ending, the only sane response to the inevitable loss of a dear friend. In between, there's a lot to learn and a lot of work to do. A dog needs care and time. He needs education, limits set, exercise, nutritious food, a warm place to sleep, a chance to express his sense of humor and his joy at being alive. To the profound sadness of most professionals who work with dog owners after the owner-pet relationship has gone astray, love is there, but little else. And as Job Michael Evans points out clearly in this important book on counseling, love, by itself, is not enough.

For the first time, dog trainers, veterinarians, breeders, anyone who tries to help dog owners in trouble, have a book to turn to—one that explains the nuts and bolts of a relatively new discipline. Though many dog trainers have always used counseling as an integral part of working with people and dogs, it didn't have a name to separate it or indicate its importance. Had they named it, people just would have made the obligatory jokes: "What do you do, get the dogs to talk about their childhoods?" "Do you do dream-interpretation? My dog runs in his sleep. What does that mean?" And on and on they'd go.

But the millions of pet dogs in our country, the billion dollar pet industry, the work now being done with autistic children, with the handicapped, in nursing homes, in prisons, all attest to the importance of the human/animal bond—and the importance of fixing it when it gets messed up. People have been giving well meaning advice about dogs for as long as people have been living with dogs, since around the time of Tyrannosaurus rex! But it wasn't until now that the necessity to counsel formally, seriously and well became a crying necessity. The harder and more complex life

9

becomes, the closer we humans live together, the less space we have to ourselves and the more pressure in our lives, the more we cling to our beloved canine pals—and the worse job we do in raising them. As a result, mixed in with the pleasure we get from our pets, we are plagued with destructiveness, biting, barking marathons, territorial marking indoors and dozens of other problems that, if not cured, inspire otherwise humane people to send their pets off to the pound.

This fascinating book, the first of its kind, will give the novice trainer the manual he needs for work in this complex and interesting field. Yet it is rich enough, detailed enough and well thought-out enough that it can offer fresh ideas and deeper understanding to the long time professional as well as the beginner.

Job Michael Evans, former training director at New Skete Monastery and now director of his own dog school, Patience of Job, in New York City, understands well the heartbreak and confusion of the dog owner in trouble who cannot understand why the genuine love he feels for his pet is not enough to make the relationship work well. His book can teach the would-be counselor how to take the client and dog step by step through the process of recognition, understanding and finally restructuring their relationship. His tools are knowledge, tact and humor. His book is an important, original contribution to the emerging field of dog psychology. I am delighted to see this material in print at last—and honored to have been asked to contribute to it.

Carol Lea Benjamin
author of *Dog Problems, Dog Tricks,*
Dog Training for Kids, and
monthly columnist, *American Kennel Gazette*

Acknowledgments

Fırsт, there is no way I can adequately express my gratitude to and admiration for the monks of New Skete with whom I was privileged to live for over eleven years. It is to them that this modest book is dedicated.

Several members of the veterinary community have been of great help to me over the years both by personal friendship and professional exchanges. I would like to thank especially Dr. Michael Fox of the Institute for the Study of Animal Problems, Humane Society of the United States, Washington, D.C.; Dr. Thomas Wolski, who originally convinced me to teach seminars in canine behavior to students from Cornell Veterinary School; Dr. R.W. Worley, South Bend Animal Clinic, South Bend, Indiana; Dr. George Glanzberg of North Bennington, Vermont; and Dr. Myrna Milani of Fitzwilliam, New Hampshire.

When I came to New York to start my own business, several members of the veterinary community helped me. I am indebted especially to Dr. Jane Bicks, whose specialty is small-animal nutrition and who was my speaking partner for several months, and to the veterinarians at Park East Animal Hospital, Dr. Lewis Berman, Dr. Paul Cavanagh, and Dr. Stephen Kritsick. My thanks also to these New York City practitioners: Dr. Malcolm Kram, Dr. Joseph Brodsky, Dr. Gerald Johnson, Dr. Howard Kessler, Dr. Adrian Alexandru and others too numerous to mention here. To all of you, my sincere thanks.

Three psychologists have helped me to understand the interplay between dog and man more fully and have helped me to learn counseling skills and I am grateful to my father, Dr. Leo Evans, Ann

Arbor, Michigan, Dr. Lynn Levo CSJ, Albany, New York and Dr. Dennis Fetko, San Diego, California. My thanks also to the famed family therapist, Virginia Satir.

The following have been my mentors in mastering training skills and gaining a deeper knowledge of dogs and I thank Carol Benjamin, Steve Lennard, Don and Joyce Arner, Jack and Wendy Volhard, Sidney Mihls, Nancy Strouss Caselman, Marie Ehrenberg, and Dr. Erich Klinghammer and Patricia Goodman of Wolf Park in Indiana.

Finally my thanks to Helen "Scootie" Sherlock, guide and mentor for many years, and to my mother, Eileen Evans in whose beautiful home in Naples, Florida, I completed this book.

1
Starting Out

WHEN I ENTERED the monastery of New Skete in 1972 I knew little or nothing about dogs. Since I come from an abnormally large family, we never had room for dogs and possibilities during college to have a canine friend were limited. But the monastery's main support came from its training and breeding programs, and I knew my work life would somehow include dogs. The dogs were literally everywhere: they slept in the monks' rooms, held down-stays around the table during dinner, followed the brothers everywhere and greeted the never-ending flow of guests. I was assigned a dog of my own, which I promptly began to indulge and spoil, despite the admonishments of the other more experienced monks. After all, who *isn't* an expert when it comes to one's dog?

But my know-it-all attitude concerning "Cita" (the dog I was currently ruining) could not withstand the authority of Brother Thomas, then in charge of the dog programs and thus of the overall handling of the dogs at the monastery. I had my first experience of dog owner counseling when he counseled *me*. He told me in no uncertain terms that I was spoiling "Cita"—rotten. He outlined how my behavior toward the dog would have to change and made sure I understood the new regulations. He then told me that "Cita" would be sent to the neighboring convent for a week, not only to expose her to women, but, basically, to get the dog away from me. I was a bad influence on my own dog. My first counseling session had ended, my beloved "Cita" shipped off to a convent.

I remember feeling distinctly grateful for the advice Brother Thomas gave me, however, and my reaction must have showed him something also for shortly afterwards he asked me to be his apprentice in dog training. At that time he was handling all the load of the training and breeding programs singlehandedly. As the monastery's work with dogs became better known, more and more dog owners began bringing their pets for training. And so I began, each day two-hour long sessions with Brother Thomas and the dogs.

When Brother Thomas died tragically in an automobile accident in 1973 the entire load fell to me. Thank God I had had the benefit of one solid year of work with him, his strong guiding hand teaching me timing and control, his even stronger spirit inspiring me. He had begun at New Skete an oral tradition of dog wisdom that continues even today, and I was grateful to have been on the receiving end of such knowledge.

Back then, Brother Thomas did little formal counseling with dog owners. But he did inaugurate extended conversations with many owners, and conducted interviews. He had that singular ability to catalog in his mind the basic data concerning the owner and dog and synthesize the information concerning the two. At that time, he used no forms for clients, although he did keep private records of dogs we trained. He taught me most of all the importance of listening. Once he remarked, "Someone should devise a form for interviewing a dog owner—make more of a science out of it." But then, like most of the brilliant dog trainers of that time, he was off again, to train another dog or whelp a litter.

Then, in 1975, someone did devise a form, make more of a science out of it. William Campbell's *Behavior Problems in Dogs* had a great impact on me and on many other trainers, not to mention veterinarians and other animal workers. Finally, here was a viable system for working with dog owners, a book detailing a totally new approach to dog training. It was a well written, funny book, and I read it three times within one week. The cryptic text reminded me of the way Brother Thomas used to talk. Yet, my identification with the book was more than emotional. On a purely rational level I knew that this was a pioneering book.

My father, a psychologist, had worked in the 1960's with the famed family therapist, Virginia Satir, and even though I was distinctly without a family of my own at the time, living in a monastery is like living in a family, and I would read her books in order to gain a better understanding of family dynamics. When I read Dr. Satir back to back with William Campbell, it occurred to me that they were talking about the same things. I began to think of a

14

synthesis of their ideas with some of my own, and this book is partially a result of that impulse.

I began to think of a book that would address the many aspects of talking with dog owners. Not just about problems like chewing, digging, and so on but about matters like euthanization (which I knew from experience had a tremendous impact on owners) and other concerns. I also felt a need for a book on *technique,* so that those who take up dog owner counseling would have a text to guide them, and have a means of deciding whether the field is for them in the first place. I believe firmly that the nature of dog training in America is changing and will continue to change dramatically over the next twenty-five years. ·What I call "straight training"—the typical hup, two, three, four obedience course will have to include some form of counseling for the dog owner. Dog owners will demand it.

So, in 1981 I began a 15-part series in *Off Lead,* the national dog training monthly. This book grew out of that series and much new information has been added. Surprisingly, the series was nominated as "Best Series" that year by the Dog Writer's Association of America, and overall reaction was good—we had broken some more ground.

Oh, "Cita" came back from the convent a much calmer dog. I was glad that in that instance I was the counselee instead of the counselor.

Finally, by way of introduction, I should mention the role of the monks' book, *How to Be Your Dog's Best Friend: A Training Manual for Dog Owners* (Little, Brown and Company, 1978). I was graced to co-author this book with the other monks. Many of the techniques detailed in that book are again stressed here, and I will refer to it throughout the pages that follow. Anyone interested in this book will find it helpful to have read *How to Be Your Dog's Best Friend* first as this volume takes many of the concepts addressed in that fine volume and explains them from the point of view of the counselor and trainer. This book is, in a sense an amplification of many of the points made in the monks' book for the lay dog owner. *The Evans Guide for Counseling Dog Owners* is inevitably a result of *How to Be Your Dog's Best Friend,* which Dr. Michael Fox called "a unique and major breakthrough in the area of animal training." This book is a companion volume to it.

2
Scope

TODAY, counseling is a diverse field, encompassing many disciplines and drawing its inspiration from many sources. No longer is counseling considered something for high school students, or a step down from psycho-therapy, or a kind of "psychiatry for the poor." Professional counseling has many branches and they reach out to include an individual's family, friends, job, attitudes and pets. Dog owner counseling is not really new. Veterinarians have been doing it for years. So have breeders and trainers. Some may feel that the idea of a book on dog owner counseling is suspect, but most feel a need for a guidebook.

People laughed at the idea of industrial psychology when it was first introduced. "Who needs it?" some asked. Yet, the complexities of job stress, tension and advancement were areas many had trouble coping with. Some said anyone who had trouble on the job and needed counseling shouldn't be working, and, in the same fashion, some in the dog fancy might say that anyone who needs an extended time to talk with a professional about their dog's behavior shouldn't have a dog. Trouble is, that would reduce the dog owning public almost to nothing.

In a recent survey conducted by the Pet Food Institute 24% of all dog owners classify themselves as "worried" owners, that is, they are concerned that their dogs are not under their control. Another 19% consider themselves "dissatisfied" owners. According to the survey this dissatisfaction would probably be alleviated if the dog was sufficiently trained or housebroken so that it no longer posed a threat or nuisance to the owner.

In short, almost one half of the dog owners in the country feel that their relationship with their dog is somehow not what it could

16

**Almost half the dog owners in the country feel that
their relationship with their dog is not what it could be.**

be. (Survey reported in *Boarding Kennel Proprietor,* January 1979, page 10.)

Dog owner counseling might be classified as a form of obedience or control training, but it must also be considered counseling, since it involves a one-to-one encounter between a professional and a client and concerns a problem. Some critics conjur up visions of dogs or owners or both prostrate on a Freudian couch, with the dog reliving its litter experiences and the owner recalling dogs owned in childhood. While the media may prefer to portray dog owner counseling this way, most dog owner counselors are "now" counselors: they are not interested in the past except insofar as it illuminates the present. They are interested in what's happening in the dog/owner relationship right *now* and solutions for problems and concerns that are pressing *now.*

Stripped of all surrounding jargon, dog owner counseling is simply another form of *training,* but the word "training" must be understood to include the owner also. A basic premise of dog owner counseling is that more is involved than simply "getting the dog in line" or "teaching the dog its place." The specialist can only study and explain areas in the dog/owner relationship that need work. As William Campbell states, "The owner alone has the power to adjust the pet's environment." Sharing these insights and giving appropriate advice takes time, close contact and mutual exchange—in short, counseling.

3

Should *You* Counsel?

D OG OWNER COUNSELING, like all forms of dog training, is essentially a *learned* skill. There is no university that gives degrees in dog owner counseling; and even if there were it is debatable whether that course of study would necessarily prepare one to counsel dog owners. In this field, hard, cold experience is the best teacher.

Courses in psychology, counseling techniques, kennel management, behavior psychology, veterinary medicine and technology and related fields might be of value and those with opportunities for these should take them. However, *lived* experience with dogs and their owners is the best teacher.

Some of the best trainers and counselors I know began as assistants in veterinary offices, simply accepting dogs from their owners, filling out forms and trotting the dogs back to the exam rooms. A year or so of this routine might drive one crazy, or it could teach many insights to the perceptive student of canine behavior and human emotions. For instance, one former veterinary assistant learned to "read" the owner's facial expressions over the course of one year. Now, when clients come to her office she knows what problems they are experiencing with their dogs before they even begin to talk about them, and often surprises them by telling them the problem in advance. ("He chews, doesn't he?")

She also learned how to take a dog from an owner so tactfully and gracefully that the dog does not realize it is being separated from its owner, even after an emotional goodbye scene.

In this field, hard, cold experience is the best teacher.

Subtleties, nuances, shades of meaning and the ability to perceive them are essential tools of the dog owner counselor's trade. An ability to see the complex nature of relationships between animals and men is essential. A love for animals is important, but an over-riding concern for the betterment of relationships is essential also. Love of a challenge, and dedication to the ideas behind responsible pet ownership are needed. If the counselor does not passionately believe in the validity of pet/human interaction, it is no sense counseling for the betterment of that relationship.

Another temptation: the Messiah Complex. This complex plagues many beginning trainers/counselors. Some wish, in ever-so-subtle ways, to dictate who gets what dog, to "protect" dogs from cruel, ineffective or just stupid owners, to "save" all dogs. It should be clear in your mind if you are involved talking with dog owners, or wish to become involved, that the job entails advising the owner on the nature of the dog/owner pact, *not* in controlling the dogs or people involved.

If your driving motivation behind desiring to work with dog owners is "love of dogs" check your interior for any traces of the "Messiah Complex"—it leads quickly to burn-out, rust-out, frustration and even despair. Love of animals is not enough for our kind of work. Indeed, love is not enough for even the rank and file pet owner. This is a point Dr. Michael Fox makes time and again in his books. Love is never enough—knowledge, understanding, compassion are the keys.

Because this type of work involves advising on the nature of a relationship we often find persons who are trained in or enamored of psychology or sociology involved with dog owner counseling. This is perfectly fine, if the person is aware of the differences between counseling human beings about human problems and concerns and counseling dog owners about canine concerns. For instance, no dog owner counselor would attempt to give advice on family matters or on personal matters, except insofar as they relate to the handling of the dog. While these matters often surface in our work, many of us are not trained to deal with them. We should refer clients needing or desiring such help to competent persons. Who should counsel? First and foremost a person who can recognize his or her limitations.

It's not necessarily true that veterinarians, breeders, class-style trainers or animal shelter personnel make the best dog owner counselors. Experience in these fields helps, and one could work in all of these areas for some time and glean enough experience in each one to integrate it successfully into his or her work. Suffice it to say that experience is essential in all of the above fields, at least to some degree.

First the prospective counselor should have a working knowledge of current veterinary theory, especially in the fields of anatomy, physiology, parasitology and neurology. You should cultivate direct contact and a working relationship with a veterinarian. We will discuss relationships between counselors and veterinarians later on.

Similarly, you should have some knowledge of genetics and of the canine youngster, including neonatal care, whelping procedures, puppy behavior and testing, litter behavior and life stages of the dog. This does *not* mean that the potential counselor should breed a litter. Visiting a professional breeder or attending seminars is much more effective—and more humane. If you want to be a dog owner counselor, train yourself immediately concerning the serious pet population explosion in this country. For anyone to breed another surplus litter for individual educational enrichment would be reprehensible.

Experience in regular obedience work is, in my opinion, the *best* preparation for the aspiring counselor. Here, after months and years on the other end of the leash, one learns what timing is, what it feels like inside the dog, how to "flow" with the dog—one learns harmony and grace. This is knowledge that then can be shared, and it is different than academic knowledge.

In fact, no one should attempt dog owner counseling without at least one year of direct field experience with dogs—and many experienced counselors would say five years of field experience. This may mean working as an assistant to an established class instructor, attending clinics, seminars and dog shows.

One of the greatest impoverished areas of many working in dog owner counseling is their failure to investigate and learn standard obedience training. A feeling develops that class-type training is somehow "beneath" them, that such trainers simply produce robots. This is certainly not the whole story and any counselor who deals with dogs must first be a skilled dog *trainer*. Because in the end, dog owner counseling is another form of training.

As a result of a certain academic syndrome prevalent in some dog owner counselors we now have within the training field a new

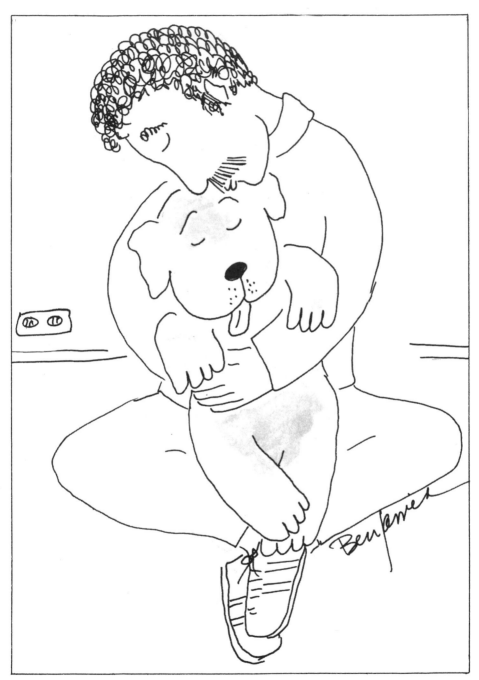

Love is not all—knowledge, understanding, compassion are the keys.

type of trainer, someone overloaded with doctrinal baggage. This person is fully acquainted with the latest psychological terms, and can rattle them off at a moment's notice, but he cannot train the heel. This person can talk sympathetically to a dog owner for hours and even solve some pressing problems, but he literally does not know how to train a dog to hold a long down without getting bitten in the process.

In fact, perhaps an unfortunate split is developing between trainers who recognize the good of dog owner counseling and those that think it is just the latest hogwash. Understandably, many trainers who may be sympathetic to the concept of counseling and who may wish to incorporate its methods into their class work are turned off by human psychiatric terminology when applied to dogs. Many times there is not the realization that most behavioral terms like shaping, flooding, altering, operating and so on apply to any species. But no doubt there has been a bit of overkill in this area especially in the writings of some specialists with a psychiatric background that preceded their involvement with dogs.

For our purposes in this book, I'll try to keep such jargon to a minimum. I am well acquainted with most of it, but my training revolved around the usual intense experience of training 5-15 dogs each day, every day for over a decade. My real love is training dogs in the field. Dog owner counseling has meant for me, a *redoubling* of effort to become proficient in *both* areas. My belief is that counseling gives the owner more time, a quantity so lacking in our world. But, I stress again, practicing dog owner counseling should in no way free the trainer from the responsibility of field work. Working directly with dogs is the only way you can get the facts directly from them.

4

Some Practical Suggestions Before You Start Out

ONE OF THE MOST INVALUABLE AIDS to becoming a good dog owner counselor is to volunteer for duty at your local humane society. At a shelter, one meets on a day-to-day basis the problem children of the pet kingdom, and a great many problem owners. One shelter worker put it this way: "The constant flow of canine personalities, and the technical difficulties they present, the variety of breed types and the range of temperaments is sometimes mind-boggling. No two days are the same." At a shelter, one sees first hand the depth of the problem of pet over-population, the drastic consequences of owner mismanagement and neglect. One learns graphically that, truly, love is *not* enough as tearful owners drop off their pets pleading that they not be euthanized, that they are really "no problem," all they need is a different home, that they were always "loved."

Attending seminars and workshops is essential. But, remember that much of the information you hear at seminars is condensed, and depending on the pace of the day, may go right over your head. If tape recording is permitted (ask in advance) make a tape, or take a notebook for memory joggers or both. Only the truly humble learn from each seminar they attend, even if some information is repetitious.

Once I spoke with a trainer of some standing after she had

attended a training seminar at a prestigious kennel. The workshop had been peppered with well-known trainers and specialists from all over the country. It had lasted four days and ran from eight a.m. to five p.m. each day. But the experience had been wasted on this woman for as she put it, "I don't know why anyone came. Everyone was trying their best to get the first word in, then trying to get the last word in. It appeared that everyone thought they knew it all already, so why attend the seminar in the first place? Just to strut their stuff, I guess!"

"Strutting the stuff" is a common ailment in the dog fancy where ego runs rampant and the crasser forms of competition sometimes seem to predominate. Perhaps it is the lack of licensing or bonafide "credentials" with which one can "prove" that he or she is competent and knowledgeable that causes such displays. It is a long climb up in the dog fancy, and "blessed are the meek" for I've certainly seen that they make the most significant and lasting contributions. Humble, open people like Helen "Scootie" Sherlock, Rachel Page Elliot, Marie Leary and the monks of New Skete come immediately to mind. I'm sure you know others who are making their own contributions without fanfare or driving ambition. While I am not downgrading healthy competition, such luminaries do inspire us all in a field that is awash with cut-throats, charlatans and outright crooks. Such souls are invaluable in a profession that is learned. Do yourself a favor: ask such a person for a day or two with them alone, even if it means joining them for travel or for simple daily chores. Then, listen and learn, and don't pick their brains for any information you can get. Just being around talented people will help you in your work. It's a process of osmosis.

One sure way to find out about your training or counseling skills is to set up a double blind situation for yourself and have your performance evaluated. Let other trainers and counselors watch you on the job. Again, this calls for a certain amount of humility and willingness to learn. It is useful to have yourself evaluated by persons in both the dog training and people helping professions. After all, the skills of a dog owner counselor border on both areas.

Most professional trainers will be happy to work with you and critique your training skills, and indeed, this is a staple feature of seminars like the Volhard Motivational Method course. There may be a fee for such a service, but you will find it well worth your money. If one is not quoted a fee, offer to pay for the trainer's time anyway.

Remember you will need to provide a dog to work with, unless the trainer wants to view you training a strange dog, which is often more useful in evaluating training talents.

With the advent of reasonably priced home video equipment another avenue for evaluation has opened. If you can have yourself taped as you train, you can then view the tape alone or with another professional. If the tape deck is equipped with a stop action switch you can stop the video the moment you make a mistake, or do something well, and highlight what you have done. The camera will provide a telling view that would otherwise not be yours. There are areas of a dog's body that are difficult or impossible to watch if you are training well, and the video will enable you to see how the dog is reacting to the training. A side point: the video camera should be operated professionally and a tripod should be used for long sequences. A poorly made video is of little value.

In evaluating counseling skills the same technique can be used. If you live near a large university with a psychology or counseling department a specially equipped room for just this purpose may be available. It may be possible to rent the room and interview a dog owner there instead of in the home or office. Professionals involved in counseling utilize this type of teaching tool time and again during their years of study. Another method is to have a counselor/trainer evaluate you by watching your interview through a one-way mirror. A third less effective method is to have a helper sit in on a training session or interview with you.

These ideas might sound outlandish to some but they do pay off. Especially in the early stages of work, seeing yourself on a video machine can help you correct negative points that may later become habits. One man I know had himself video-taped in a counseling session and went back to work in a boarding kennel situation. "I'm good, real good with dogs," he said, "but the interview showed me something about myself—I constantly interrupted the dog owner— I'm just not a good listener!" And another trainer noted, "Until I saw the video I had no idea I crowded the dog like that on the heel, nor did I realize how clumsy I am in placing the dog into a down. On the other hand, I felt pretty good when I saw the dog I was training smiling as we heeled along—I thought I could feel the smile but I wasn't sure and didn't want to break the nice pattern we had going, but on the video the dog looked like I had just told him the funniest joke in the world!"

5

Getting Set Up

You are offering time

Aϩκ PROFESSIONAL DOG PEOPLE how
they had to gain the bulk of their knowledge and they will tell you
about hectic dog shows where someone dropped one measly nugget
of advice which they happened to remember upon getting home, of
poorly run seminars where the sound system made it impossible to
hear the talks, which were unprepared and even more uninformative
anyway, and a host of other dismal tales. "I learned everything I
know myself" is a common statement. Wendy Volhard, who tries to
run quiet, structured and informative clinics once visited me at the
monastery and remarked, "It's so wonderful to sit here with you and
talk in the midst of this silence. Dog people for the most part are
usually running or eating when they discuss dogs—or anything for
that matter, *if* they discuss anything other than dogs!"

The situation at the typical veterinary office isn't much better.
Behind the facade of the quiet, sedate waiting room, all hell may be
breaking loose. The professional veneer of courtesy and calm hides
the fact that Dr. Vet is three clients behind, got out of surgery late
that morning and hasn't had his 10:30 a.m. coffee break, nor have his
assistants. If it's harried for the practitioner, it's worse for the clients,
who leaf through magazines for extended periods of time, waiting
ten minutes or longer for their turn in the exam room. The client is
perfectly aware that others, too, are waiting and is eager to vacate
the premises. If the dog is having a problem, the client will take a
shot at getting some help from the veterinarian, but isn't too
hopeful.

There is no compelling reason to expect either of the two

above-mentioned situations to change for the better in the near future. With a predicted shortage of veterinarians and a plethora of pets with medical problems, behavior problems necessarily take a back seat. The fact that many veterinarians simply do not have any training or interest in canine behavior doesn't help matters.

This is where you come in. The dog owner counselor's most precious offering is *time and skill.* The very fact that the counselor makes time for the client is important. Harried dog people can't do it—the recreational vehicle needs tuning before the shove-off for the next show. The local veterinarian isn't skilled or interested, usually. But because you offer time doesn't mean you want to sit all day and talk about Fido's problems. Clients must be told at the onset of the interview:

1) Time is available.
2) How much time is available.

Remember—dog owners are notorious for going on and on with dog stories. Professional dog people are sometimes chronic talkers and lay dog owners are no better. Many lay owners suffer from over-verbalization with both dogs and humans (we will discuss this in detail in a later chapter). Be careful! Distraught or upset clients are capable of rambling aimlessly and of filling literally hours of your time.

Setting Time Limits

This should be done before meeting the client. It is conveniently included at the end of the initial phone call or tacked on the end of an appointment letter. Say something like, "Good, we'll plan to get together at 10 a.m. on Thursday morning, August the 10th. I hope we can start right at 10 as I want to be sure to have a full hour to spend with you." When the actual meeting occurs, you set the time limit again, "I'm glad we're together. We have a full hour (or half hour, two hours). Let's get started and see what we can accomplish."

Clients will often speed up the whole interview process when they realize that only a certain amount of time is available. Instead of giving you a twenty-minute description of how Tippy didn't eat all of her Gaines Burgers that morning they will get right to the heart of the problems that bother them. I often have clients fill out certain forms before the interview, but I do not include this time in the interview time. If forms are involved, readjust the time schedule to include at least 15-20 minutes for filling out forms. Remember, your client is not acquainted with your forms as you are, and different people write at different speeds.

Naturally, if the counselor indicates that an hour will be available, he or she is ethically bound to provide an uninterrupted hour of time for that client. Juggling clients by running between two or more interview rooms (or homes, as the case may be!) is unacceptable. Answering the phone during an interview is tacky. If you interview clients in their homes, ask them to turn off the television and radio, and to take the phone off the hook unless an emergency call is due.

If you have a waiting room and know clients will be waiting or in the unfortunate event that they "stack up"—usually because one client is late, it's a good idea to help them utilize the time by providing good reading material. Xeroxed copies of dog behavior articles, an attractive portfolio, copies of *Off Lead* and veterinary magazines can be left there, or given directly to clients.

Room Set-Up

You'd be well advised to stick to the lessons learned by counselors of all persuasions. Here are some basic hints on room set-up:

1) The room should be well-lit and ventilated. Furniture should be comfortable but not opulent, and positioned so that the counselor and client can face each other. Direct light should not shine on the counselor's or client's face. If you go into the home for your work, try to modify the environment as much as possible using these guidelines.

2) Counseling from behind a desk adds a remote air to the session. It is too cold and contrived for this kind of work.

3) Furniture should include a coffee table or side table, with ash trays if smoking is allowed.

4) Some counselors prefer to sit in a specific chair or spot, either because it aids their comfort or sets them off as the helper. If this is

the case, it is best to indicate this. Putting your notebook on the seat of the chair you intend to occupy usually makes this clear. The alternative is to scramble to get the chair you want, or ask an erring client to move. If you counsel in the home, take the seat offered to you, but don't hesitate to ask to sit elsewhere if you think it would be better for the interview.

5) Obviously, sit and talk, do not stand.

6) If you plan to talk with a large group, make sure there are enough seats for all. In the home, invite family members who are "hanging around" to come in and have a seat—as they are a distraction to you and to your client if they hover about in the hallways.

7) If charts or diagrams are to be used the participants must be positioned so that they can easily see what is being shown.

Here are some more tips specifically concerning dog owner counseling gleaned from my own experience:

1) Flooring is important. Many veterinarians install tile floors only to find the lack of traction they provide can make managing nervous dogs quite difficult. Regular carpet, on the other hand, picks up dog and cat hair easily and is difficult to clean. Good quality indoor/outdoor carpet, preferably in tiles that can be lifted off the floor and cleaned individually is excellent for traction and cleanliness.

2) Do not use furniture adorned with tufts or buttons. Furniture with fringes will soon be fringeless. Dog-proof the area as much as you can!

3) Position the furniture so that there is enough room for the dog, too. This means adequate space around your chair and the client's chair. If you are going into the client's home and do not have any possibility of rearranging the room, study the unstable items around you so that if the dog jumps on you or attempts to get in your lap (or charge you, pummel you, molest you, whatever) there will not be a precious heirloom smashed in the process.

4) Doors that open into the room are good. Doors that swing both ways are best. Nothing is worse than an interview that begins with a dog-door mishap.

5) Coffee or tea is nice. It relaxes many clients and takes the air of

starchiness away. If you are offered something to drink in a client's home, accept it graciously, but never accept an alcoholic beverage while on the job.

6) Whether in your own setting or out on the road, have a supply of good dog treats available. Remember, if a strange dog is to accept a treat from you, it should be a couple of notches above what is usually offered. Cheese usually works. But ask the client if you can give the treat, and don't give a treat if you suspect that less than one hour later you will be advising the client to cut back on treats. A side benefit is that a treat keeps the dog quiet if the dog is "attending" the interview.

7) Have pooper-scoopers and cleaning aids nearby in case of an emergency if you are using your own facility, and if an accident occurs in the client's home use the time to make more notes or entertain the dog while the clean-up takes place. Don't make a big thing out of accidents; they have a funny side.

6

Meeting People and Dogs

AT FIRST GLANCE meeting a person or a dog would appear to be no problem, but it's amazing how many people make a royal mess out of both routines. For your work, a wonderful first impression is absolutely necessary. You must strive to have a successful first meeting with each client and dog you meet, so some coaching may be in order here.

First, the humans. This species is terribly sensitive. For the dog person, meeting humans is often a terrible task while meeting dogs is like meeting kinfolk. But besides the usual tension involved in the introductory process, you must also set yourself off as a helper and guide while at the same time openly offering to be of service. The family therapist, Virginia Satir, has some excellent observations in an article titled "When I Meet a Person":

> I would like to explain what goes on in me when I think about using myself as a helper to another person. The person would not be coming to me unless they had some kind of pain or some kind of problem that they wanted to solve. In some way I feel them as having said to themselves, "We've reached the end of our ability to cope, and we are searching for some way to cope better."

> When people are in need or having some kind of problem, their manifestation of themselves—the way they look and sound and talk—can be pretty ugly, pretty beautiful or pretty painful. But underneath all this I see the living human who, I feel, if he were in touch with the life he is and has, would use himself differently. So that means that with every human being I encounter, I mentally take off his outside and try to see his inside. . .

> No changes can be made in people unless they feel themselves as having

worth, and I as a helper become the first means by which a person comes in touch with his own feelings of worth. So my meeting with this person is the beginning of this. I stand in front of you and reach out my hand to you at arm level. As I reach for your hand and you give it to me, I feel the connection. At that moment in time, I am looking at you, and for that moment there is no one else in the world except you and me. A smile accompanies this, and my smile is saying "hello" to you and to your life as a representation of all life. It is like building a platform or base from which we are going to go. I do not start out the session with a discussion of the problem, but rather make this basic connection on a human level with everybody. Of course people are coming in for some help; and if they knew what sort of help they needed, they would probably be doing it themselves and not seeking me. They have come to the end of their coping and they want some help, but probably all that they are aware of is that they have pain.

When you meet someone, make direct eye contact with them, and continue to look at them as they talk. Especially if you intend to lecture them later on the importance of eye contact between dog and handler be sure you manifest it yourself in your own interactions. I usually begin by making some kind of small talk about the weather, or about the interior of the home. But a sure-fire way to the dog owner's heart is to compliment the dog. If you think about it, there is something beautiful about every dog. You can mention that it is a fine specimen of the breed. Perhaps the coat looks especially good. If not, the tail might be wagging. Even if the dog is trying to attack you, you can compliment the dog's dentition. Say *something* kind about the dog's appearance, and mean it.

Meeting the dog is usually much less tense, but many of the same ground rules apply. First, get down on the dog's level, extend your hand and give the dog a quick ruff-ruff around the neck. Make your overture quick but affectionate and don't rev the dog up into a frenzy. If the dog is already off the wall and mauling you, return the affection but stand quickly, and raise your arms up near your chest and feign passivity, get seated and begin work as soon as you can.

When meeting an aggressive dog, all the rules change. Don't try to go out to these dogs. They are angry at you, and if you are within ten feet of them, as far as they are concerned you have invaded their turf and are the enemy. Look over the dog not at it, and do not feel that you must make contact with the dog to "prove" anything to the owner. You must wisely pace physical contact with such animals, evaluating the situation as it develops.

34

If you think about it, there is something beautiful about every dog.

I feel strongly that barring truly dangerous situations you should try to make physical contact with both dog and owner from the outset—after all, these are the two beings you will be working with. But not all trainers feel this way. One urban trainer, a victim of many dog bites, now says, "I don't pet any dog during the first meeting," and other trainers see little importance in the interaction they have with the owner. But your first impression is very important indeed—it is, as Satir explains, the "platform" on which all of your future work will be built.

7

The Interview: Should the Dog Be Present?

SHOULD THE DOG be present when the initial interview is conducted? If you work out of your own office, you can determine this for yourself with the guidelines that follow. If you work in the client's home you'll have little choice—the dog may be not only present but may be in your lap, helping you take notes.

Many trainers prefer that the dog be present so that they can read the dog's interaction with its owner. The dog will usually be somewhat unruly at first, and this often gives invaluable insights as to just how the owner elicits obedience from the dog, if at all. Since the dog will often regard the interviewer with suspicion, unease, fear and occasionally with perfect equanimity, the trainer gets a kind of preview as to just how the training segments will progress.

If the dog is present, obvious questions pertaining to size, breed type, coat quality, sex and character are automatically answered. If the dog is a mix the trained eye can usually ascertain the components of the mix readily if the dog is on the scene. Finally, the exact physical condition can be evaluated on the spot.

Some trainers like to see the dog and owner together because they feel the client expects it. "After all, you're here to help the dog, not me," said one client. "So why shouldn't you see the dog and me at the same time?" There is a point here, but it is interesting to note who is dictating the terms of the interview. Clients often feel "on-the-

Dog owners tend to lie about their pets more if the dog is present.

spot" if they are interviewed without the dog present. They feel that their behavior, not the dog's, is being evaluated. This embarrasses them. Trouble is, they are partially right.

When working out of an office, I prefer to see the owner first, then the dog. I instruct the client to leave the dog in the car when they arrive. This is done over the phone when the initial appointment is made. The owner arrives, dogless, at the office, and then the interview starts. Occasionally the client will indicate, "My dog can't stay in the car—he'll chew it to shreds, that's why I'm coming to you," and then the dog will be temporarily settled in a kennel where he cannot do any damage.

There are several reasons for this approach. Primarily, the rationale is practical, since it is often impossible to conduct a fact-finding interview with an unruly dog on the scene. For instance, most clients cannot fill out the necessary forms while trying to restrain a wild dog with one hand. Secondly, since the dog has often just experienced a long car trip, and is dragged immediately into a strange environment and forced to meet new people, some dogs will urinate or defecate and some of the more unstable types will emit their "fear gland" causing considerable problems for owner and trainer.

Client Deception

If the dog is allowed to attend (or hold court, rule, crash, control or whatever verb is appropriate) the initial interview the owner may find himself or herself defending, denying or even lying about the animal when, in fact, if the dog was not present, the owner would feel no such obligation. In over ten years of interviewing owners, I've seen this phenomenon continually. The plain fact is, dog owners tend to lie about their pets more if the dog is present and less when the dog is absent!

We have to realize that as interviewers and trainers we often put a dog owner in a defensive position by virtue of the very help they are seeking. It takes a certain amount of humility to admit that one needs help, especially in an area like training a dog. Doesn't the popular folklore say that *anyone* can train a dog—a person would have to be really *stupid* to need help in such a task. And many clients will make it subtly or not-so-subtly clear that it's the dog that needs help, not them.

My advice is to eliminate the dog from the initial interview.

The counselor has to make it clear, subtly or not-so-subtly, that the client does indeed need help, and he or she may be able to obtain it much more effectively if the dog is not present for the initial interview. For example, once one of my co-workers intercepted a client in front of my office who had forgot to leave her dog in the car and had the Bullmastiff in tow. The co-worker explained that the dog should be left in the car and would be evaluated after the owner was interviewed. "Oh, you mean after you evaluate *me*," the owner cracked, and the co-worker replied, "That's about right." Both laughed and then struck up a short conversation about the dog. Later, when I compared mental notes with this fellow trainer we were struck with the discrepancies in the separate reports we had been given about the same dog by the same person. When the dog was present, during the encounter on the sidewalk, the report was full of commendations and pride. Later interviewed minus the dog in the office, the description of the dog was mingled with condemnations, accusations and apologies. The pivotal factor seemed to be the presence or absence of the creature being discussed!

My advice, then, is to eliminate the dog from the initial interview. Care must be taken not to insult the client. Usually a tactful explanation like, "I want you to be able to concentrate completely on telling me about your dog, and that might be easier for you if you don't have to manage the dog at the same time. You can leave the dog in the car or we can settle the dog in a kennel for awhile if you prefer." If the client insists that they want the dog nearby when they talk, there is probably little sense arguing the matter.

If you train in homes, there are some options available to you. Dr. Dennis Fetko, who works in San Diego, asks to take the dog out for a private walk, so that he can evaluate the dog independently of the owner, and sometimes the dog can be left outdoors during the interview. Another option is to take the dog for a quick evaluative session while the owner fills out the necessary interview and data forms. Still another possibility that often presents itself is to meet the dog and owner and then tactfully suggest that the dog be taken for a quick stroll by another family member. If a dog becomes totally unruly or aggressive while you are trying to conduct an interview, don't hesitate to ask the owner to put the dog in another area. It is vitally important that the interview proceed correctly, for it is the center of the counseling process as we will see.

8

The Interview:
Working with Forms

LET'S DELVE DEEPER into the interview process, which is the main creative factor that distinguishes dog owner counseling from other forms of canine training. I have seen a myriad of forms used by trainers and specialists from coast to coast. These come to me via mail and sometimes are presented to me during seminars. People usually want to know if I think their form is a good form. My answer is whatever works for you is good. But some kind of interview form is necessary to dog owner counseling for the following reasons:

1) It forces the trainer to ask appropriate questions.

2) It enables the client to provide all necessary information.

3) It helps the counselor assemble the information provided and formulate an approach to problem areas.

There are two ways of handling the interview forms when actually working with them. You can fill them out by asking the clients questions, or you can give the form to the clients and have them fill it out and go over the information they provide with them. A great many counselors prefer the first approach as it enables them to have more control over the interview process and to make private notations as the client talks.

In the second method, you must be sure that you provide enough time for your clients to fill out the form. I usually use the second approach as I feel it gives the clients some measure of control in describing problems they experience with their dogs and a chance to state what they have attempted to control those problems. Also once a client puts down something in black and white we have it for the record and it serves to give the client a new perspective, too.

One tip on interview forms, especially if you prefer the second approach in which the client fills out the form for you: never go over the front of an 8½ x 11 inch sheet of paper. After that people just quit. Do not confront the dog owner with five pages of forms asking them to catalog every aspect of their dog's behavior in writing—they might oblige! Remember, you have to read the forms also. But most will quit if the form is too lengthy, no matter how vital they think the information is. The form is a general survey of the interaction between the dog and owner, not a journal of the dog owner's (or dog's) feelings and thoughts.

Design the form *you* feel comfortable with—even if, at first you have to work with forms out of books or magazines. With the advent of cheap xerox facilities, it's relatively easy to revise your forms as you see fit. Two good sample forms accompany this chapter. One is from *Behavior Problems in Dogs,* by William Campbell (reprinted by special permission of American Veterinary Publications, 1975, page 65) and another was developed by Pam Lauritzen and appeared in the January/February 1981 issue of *Groom and Board* magazine (permission to reprint also granted). The form I like to use is modeled after Campbell's form, but is designed to be filled out by the client. I frequently add and subtract questions. One important question I ask at the end of the form is "Are you willing to accept praise and/or criticism from us of your handling of your dog and cooperate with any recommendations we may make?" The client then checks yes or no. Why it may seem like a highly rhetorical, even somewhat insulting question, most clients do not take it that way. Many circle "yes" and add "Please!" or "wholeheartedly!" or some such adjective. In ten years of using the form, I only had two people circle "no." One person had a strange sense of humor and did it as a joke to see what my reaction would be: I tried to see the humor. Another person really meant no. "It's the dog that needs recommendations, not me," he stated bluntly, but I did not train his dog. The client must adopt a learner's stance, a listener's stance in order to get anything out of dog owner counseling. In no sense is the *dog* being counseled. The dog is being trained, as is the owner, but only the owner is counseled.

Behavior Fact Sheet

Date __10/12/74__ Time __3:45__ to __4:00__ Breed __SHEP MIX__ Ⓜ F N Age __2 YRS.__

Client __MARY KARNAK (RALPH)__ Dog __BARNEY__

Address __17439 PONCE ST__ City __CANOGA PARK__ State __CA__ Zip __91364__

Problem:
- ✔ Housesoils ✔ Jumps up ✔ Aggressive ___ Runs away ___ Shy
- ___ Chews ✔ Unruly (✔) Bites ✔ No obey ___ Pica
- ___ Digs ___ Barks ___ Fights ___ Howls ___ Coprophagia

Other: __Unruly with guests: vicious, barks — was put out at 14 weeks__

Problem notes: __particularly unruly with owner when she is alone with pet — jumps__
(Age noted-locale-situation-frequency-etc.)
__on client — dog possible biter in stress — poor behavior since a puppy__

Corrections to date: __Scold (mary) - Spank/beat (ralph) - put out (both)__

Dog's reactions: __growls at her — snarls at him__

Age dog obtained: __8 weeks__ From: __Newspaper ad__ Price: __$15.—__

Litter behavior: __not seen__

Housetraining method __Scold/spank__ Other training: __Sits for treats__

Where sleep? __Bedroom floor__ In house other times? __Yes - all over__ (where?)

Bathed? __NO__ Brushed? __seldom__ Play periods? __seldom (dog is unruly)__ (Who - how)

Last vet. check: __at 1½ years__ Purpose __DHL__ Outcome __OK__

Other: __Roundworms at 8 weeks ē 5 months__

Diet __Kibble__ Daily feeds: ① 2 3 Who feeds? __client__

Quantity __12 cups__ Supplements __tidbits, scraps__

Family data: Ⓜ S D Children __presently 3 mos pregnant__ Other __—__

Occupation(s): __client = homemaker ; spouse = marriage counselor__

Other pets? __None__

Recommendations: __Feed 2x daily ½ chicken + 2 cups meal + Vitamin__
__Don't punish! Teach to come, go, stay — use SRX for jumping__
__Keep inside - act "jolly" with visitors 2 x daily — get pet door!__

Case outcome __Excellent — No problems after 5th week__ Date __11/31/74__

Notes: __Both owners attitudes excellent after consultation.__

Send aid literature? __Yes — Biting case study__

Sample Behavior Interview Form (from *Behavior Problems in Dogs*)

44

DOG'S PROFILE

SECTION I—BIOGRAPHICAL

OWNER'S NAME _____

ADDRESS _____

PHONE (home) _____ (business) _____

VETERINARIAN _____ VET'S PHONE _____

DOG'S NAME _____ (AGE) _____

MEDICATION _____ (WHAT KIND) _____

WHEN LAST GROOMED _____ (REACTION) _____

WAS THE DOG GROOMED BY PROFESSIONAL _____ OWNER _____

HOW OFTEN IS THE DOG GROOMED (BRUSHED, BATHED) AT HOME _____

WHAT GROOMING PROCEDURE IS USED _____

_____

SECTION II—MEDICAL HEALTH PROBLEMS

Seizures _____ Specify _____

Heart Disease _____ Specify _____

Blind _____ Deaf _____ Injuries _____

Allergies _____ Specify _____

Ear Infection _____ Spayed/Neutered _____

Others _____

_____

SECTION III—SOCIAL ORDER (Dominant/Submissive, Leader/Sub.)

DOES DOG RESPOND TO NAME WHEN CALLED _____ __

IS DOG HOUSE TRAINED _____ WHAT PROCEDURE USED _____

HOW DOES DOG REACT TO STRANGERS _____

DOES DOG URINATE WHEN APPROACHED _____

DOES DOG INDULGE IN SELF-MUTILATION _____

DOES DOG RESPOND TO OWNER'S DIRECTION _____

_____

SECTION IV—NERVOUS SYSTEM TYPE

IN STRESS SITUATION (new situation, strangers, left alone, confinement) DOES DOG REACT:

Wildly Active _____ Active _____ Poised, Assured _____ Reserved _____

Withdrawn (lethargic, stiff) _____

_____

SECTION V—DOMESTIC

WHAT TYPE GAMES ARE PLAYED _____

WHAT HIGHLIGHTS DOG'S DAY _____

FEEDING SCHEDULE _____

HAS DOG BITTEN ANYONE _____

WHAT WERE CIRCUMSTANCES _____

WHO ADMINISTERS PUNISHMENT _____

WHAT TYPE OF PUNISHMENT _____

_____

SECTION VI

RECOMMENDATION: __ _____

_____

From "PROBLEM DOG HANDLING" by Pam Lauritzen · · Groom & Board, Jan./Feb. 1981.

Sample Behavior Interview Form

In actuality, such a question simply asks the owner to adopt the same attitude that most dogs, if properly handled, adopt toward training—an open and willing attitude. Isn't it ironic that we even have to ask such a question? How wonderful it would be if most humans could adopt the same mind-set of most dogs: a distinct willingness to please, a desire to learn, openness, honesty.

9

The Interview: Characteristics of Dog Owners

SHOULD WE CLASSIFY dog owners in order to evaluate them? Yes! While classification might be a crude method in some ways, it is the only way the beginning owner counselor can get a handle on the type of person he or she is working with. One of the most helpful listings is William Campbell's listing in chapter two of *Behavior Problems in Dogs*. It is included in this chapter.

While Campbell's listing is comprehensive (not to mention funny) it is long and somewhat complex. I prefer a simpler typology which I have developed from Virginia Satir's book *Peoplemaking* (Science and Behavior Books, 1972). While Mrs. Satir is dealing with human families, her work can be easily applied to dog owner counseling and the stresses involved in dealing with a problem dog. For instance in her more technical manual *Conjoint Family Therapy* (also Science and Behavior Books) she introduces the concept of the "IP" or Identified Patient—essentially the one in the family that is "causing all the trouble" or that at least the others in the family consider the source of conflict. I was acquainted with this book as a young boy because Mrs. Satir worked with my own psychologist father. I would sneak down into his office and read her manual and articles in psychological journals—often to understand the interactions within my own family. Later, when heavily involved

Owner Characteristic	Relationship to the Dog
Domineering-physical	Insists on total subservience and uses excessive force and/or punishment to gain obedience.
Domineering-vocal	Wants total subservience and uses vocal volume or stern tone for obedience.
Seductive-physical	Tries to gain responses through coaxing and/or fondling the dog.
Insecure-permissive	Wants the dog's love and loyalty but avoids any form of discipline for fear of losing either or both.
Ambivalent	This produces a state of mixed emotions about the animal which leads to problems.
Paranoid	Endows the dog with emotional and intellectual capabilities which are unique to humans. This type consistently misinterprets the dog's behaviorisms, and usually already "knows" all the reasons for the problem behavior.
Naive	Knows little or nothing about dogs and often follows everyone's advice, no matter how outrageous.
Logician	Uses common-sense methods, even in the face of undesirable results.
Intractable	Displays either extreme rigidity or elasticity of attitude in response to consultative guidance; therefore is impractical as a potential force in solving the problem.
Children	See following text.

From "BEHAVIOR PROBLEMS IN DOGS" by William E. Campbell, American Veterinary Publications, 1975, Chapter 2

A Sample List of Owner Characteristics

in dog training I again picked up her books and read *Conjoint Family Therapy* envisioning a problem dog as the "IP." It worked perfectly—her techniques could be used ideally in dog owner counseling as well as in family therapy. Dogs were wonderful "IP's"—they were usually identified as causing all the trouble and the counselor's job is to show the family that the trouble proceeds not from one individual but from the relationships between all individuals with the "IP" and with each other. I could tell you more about it here but I'd like you to see for yourself. Get a copy of this book and read it substituting the name of any problem dog you know wherever the text reads "IP."

Patterns of Communication

Another contribution Mrs. Satir makes is to delineate certain patterns of communication that occur between persons. I developed her system into a typology to characterize the patterns of communication between dog owners and their dogs. They are: *placating, blaming, computing* and *distracting*. These are near-universal patterns of communication people use with each other *and* with their dogs in order to avoid the threat of rejection and elicit obedience or cooperation.

1) *Placate* so that the other person or the dog doesn't get mad, or in an attempt to get obedience or cooperation.

2) *Blame* so the other person or dog will regard you as strong.

3) *Compute* with the resultant message that you consider the possibility of bad behavior harmless.

4) *Distract* so that you just ignore the behavior as though it were not there.

All of Campbell's categories can be listed under one of these headings. We thus have a simpler classification system you may find useful. If you fit Campbell's characteristics into the Satir system you come up with this:

Placating:	*Blaming:*
Seductive-physical	Domineering-physical
Insecure-permissive	Domineering-vocal
Naive	

Computing:	*Distracting:*
Logician	Ambivalent
Intractable	Intractable
Paranoid	

Use whichever typology you wish or create your own, but remember you will need some classification system, especially when you are just beginning dog owner counseling. But, don't pigeon-hole a client into one or more sets of responses or you may not be able to help them. A rare client will not fit *any* category. And some will fit several. When you are beginning, use the classification system as a guide until you can identify types of owners without any help.

The Placater

. . . is basically PASSIVE. The vast majority of problem dog owners are placaters. They react passively to events in their dog's life and sometimes to events in their own lives. They are either afraid or ignorant of how to take an active role in solving behavioral problems. The placater always talks in an ingratiating way, trying to please, apologizing. They are usually *over-verbal* with their dogs. They are often *over-verbal* with the counselor. They talk *too much* in long whiny sentences.

The placater tries to elicit obedience out of the dog by bribing, often with food, by cajoling ("C'mon, lie down, will ya? Please? C'mon, you know what would make me happy, C'mon, pleeze, pleeeze?"). While this dog owner knows that he or she needs help in handling the dog, they will rarely blame the dog for bad behavior ("He's really *good,* he just gets nervous and bites, that's all . . . it's probably my fault . . . if I had only completed that obedience course everything would be different, I know it's my fault"). Unless the counselor is skilled, the placater will also try to placate the counselor ("I know I've failed, just tell me what to do, I'll do anything, really, anything").

How to Help the Placater:

1) EDUCATE—always our basic job. Pay special attention to educating the client in voice tonality, caution them on over-verbalization and whining. Make your criticisms gentle and to the

THE PLACATER

point. Often using the third person works: "A person who talks too much is in trouble with a dog. They come from a very silent genetic background. Think about wolves—except for their group howls they live in silence. A dog won't understand a person who is a wall of sound."

2) Do not harshly criticize or condemn the placating owner. The placater will simply *agree* with you and placate you and the dog more ("Everything you're saying is 100% right—I've spoiled him, I know, and I'm a failure"). You must inspire confidence in the owner ("I've worked with this problem so many times before, you shouldn't feel alone or hopeless—let's see what we can do working together").

3) Some chronic placaters will continue, despite your best efforts, to bootlick, blame themselves, whine. Check your approach, and if the whining gets really bad, tell the client how they are coming off to you and possibly to the dog.

4) Remember, most dogs take extreme advantage of placating behavior because they see it and hear it as submissive. The placating owner who owns a leader-type dog is in serious trouble.

The Blamer

. . . is a fault finder, a dictator, a boss. He acts superior with his dog and possibly with you. A great many professional men and women, otherwise highly educated, will fall into this category. The voice is hard, tight, often shrill and loud. This person is also over-verbal with the dog but in a loud, bossy way. They will come into the interview and *announce* what the problem is and exactly *who* is causing it. Be careful, the blaming is first focused on the dog, but the tables can be easily turned and the blaming focused on you.

The blamer begins sentences with the *dog's* name ("Rover chews . . . Rover knows he's done wrong . . . Rover just does it for spite . . . *He's* a bad dog . . . *He* gets into everything . . . *He* never listens). Watch for words like "never," "always," and "absolutely."

These people will often present a problem to you with an attitude of, "OK, what are you going to do about it?" They are very frequently over-physical and hard with their dogs. The blamer is not really interested in finding out how you work or in finding out about

THE BLAMER

anything. The blamer is only interested in pushing weight around and blaming the dog and everyone else who handles the dog including, possibly, you.

A classic case of a blamer was described in *How to Be Your Dog's Best Friend.* I met this client during my years in the monastery:

> One man wanted to know if we could train his cocker spaniel to lie down in response to a cough. The gentleman explained that he wanted "complete control" over his dog, and that he didn't want to have to bother giving the cocker a verbal command, but thought that an "ahem-type" cough should do the trick. He then demonstrated by clearing his throat suggestively. He never praised the dog verbally or physically. "My family had plenty of dogs," he explained, "and none of them needed to be hugged every two seconds." The children in the family sat rigid throughout the interview, contributing little.
>
> We explained that dogs usually need verbal commands and hand signals in order to clearly understand what is asked of them. The cough idea was not possible.
>
> At this point the wife chimed in for the first time during the interview, agreeing with us that a vocal command was necessary—but before she could finish her sentence the husband shot a silencing glance at her, clearing his throat in the same suggestive manner!

This is the classic blaming owner—and you will often be able to identify them more quickly if family members are present or if the dog is cavorting around causing trouble. I can tell them twelve miles away—they always seem to carry themselves like John Wayne, although I hasten to add that not all blamers are men.

As a side point, let's note that blaming is a stance poor counselors and trainers take. They will blame the client publicly ("You know, you are the source of all this dog's problems!"). This is an unwise approach and bound to backfire ("Look buster, I didn't come here to hear what a bad dog owner I am"). A certain extremely popular English trainer has distilled the questionable art of blaming her students into a science, publicly berating them over nationwide television. She scolds them for every infraction of her rules, repositions their hands, and generally makes them feel like two cents. The students take it because she is overwhelmingly loving with the dogs and because, of course, they have to get the dogs trained. Dogless observers think the whole process is hilarious—but I doubt the participants in the class do.

How to Help the Blamer:

1) Slow the client down. Make them sit. Talk slowly and they will too. Talk softly. Get the dog out of the room and they will blame it less.

2) Indicate *tactfully* that you notice the blaming ("Can I check something with you? You seem to be putting a lot of the blame on the dog, but maybe the dog's problems aren't that simple; what do you think?").

3) Educate the client but *don't* promise anything. Promising a blamer is a quick way of hanging yourself. In really bad cases, terminate the interview.

The Computer

. . . is very correct, very reasonable, with little feeling. He or she is calm, cool and collected. This owner could be compared to an actual computer. The voice is often dry, flat. Often commands are given to the dog in a monotone or using big words ("As I look at you, Rover, I see a recalcitrant dog, one that should be lying down"). Of course most dogs just think this is hilarious.

The computer carefully chooses words and will often try to "one-up" you in psychological jargon, as they think that because your work borders on psychiatric therapy that this will impress you. This client will often have great difficulty mastering obedience techniques. Since they are often very rigid physically, the hand motions and body positions necessary in good training will be difficult as will verbal animation and any display of praise.

Unfortunately, due to a misreading of training books or a misunderstanding of the tenets of good training, some computer owners think that this response is the *ideal* in their relationship with their dog: say the right words, show no feeling, don't react.

How to Help the Computer:

1) Because the computer owner is rigid physically and cannot move about in training, he or she must see *you* in action with the dog. The computer must see you praise the dog. This is one instance where it actually helps to take the dog from the owner and let the owner watch you work. Don't be surprised if the dog is sullen and

THE COMPUTER

unresponsive. They've probably been raised so stoically they wouldn't know how to respond to praise if they heard it—but even the worst cases eventually respond to enough bubbles.

2) Other than the witness value of letting the client see you work, there's little you can do with such rigid souls. Those of us accustomed to acting crazy with dogs will find this type of person a real trial. They are duds. Stick with it. Often the person *wants* to break out of that tight shell and is willing to use the dog to do so. Asking the computer to simply *run* with the dog for a mile each day will often loosen things up between owner and dog.

The Distractor:

. . . never makes a response to the point. Whatever he or she says is always irrelevant to what anyone else is saying or doing, including the dog. You get a dizzy feeling when you are around this type. The dog will often be extremely hyperactive in response to this handling. The voice is very singsong, going up and down ("Ooops there he goes, Watch it, cup of coffee, oops, boom, well time to go to the store!"). This type of person often tries to do several things at once and may be physically uncoordinated. The erratic body language is very confusing to the dog and makes training and discipline difficult.

The distractor will often ignore your questions during the interview or come back with a response on a different subject. They may take a piece of imaginary lint off your garment, or untie their shoelaces and then tie them, light another cigarette before the one they are smoking has burned out, and other oddities. In handling the dog they will praise and discipline at the same time, completely ignore the dog, forget the dog's name, or call the dog by several names. Occasionally they will not have chosen a name for the dog.

How to Help the Distractor:

1) The distractors may seem totally crazy but they are not. They may have very ambivalent feelings about having the dog in their lives and the bad behavior complicates these feelings. They do not know how to relate to others. One way to help is to let the client work with a *trained* dog, perhaps your own, that will respond correctly even to poor handling. This will show the client what is possible in training.

THE DISTRACTOR

2) This person often needs time away from the dog. They have too many things they are trying to pull together and the dog gets lost in the crush. You can suggest boarding the dog with you for awhile, if possible.

3) Talk very slowly, calmly, deliberately.

As dismal as the overall situation may sound, there are good dog owners around, and there is a final response that marks the happy dog/owner relationship—the Leveling Response.

In this response all of the messages are going the same way, whether the client is talking to the dog or to the counselor. The voice is reasonable, controlled, and gives commands that match the body expressions, the facial expressions and the tone of voice. The relationship between the dog and owner is free, open and honest. The dog clearly views the owner as the Alpha figure in its life and responds accordingly—and happily.

From what I've seen in counseling dog owners:

50% *placate* their dogs, saying yes or please regardless of whatever else they want to do or think should be done.

30% *blame* their dogs, and overpunish, chase, scream, shout, discipline in the wrong way, blame the dog for everything and anything no matter what they really think or feel about the pet.

15% *compute* and have little or no feeling for their dogs, or at least behave that way and would like others to think they feel that way.

½% *distract* and behave in such a way that they seem to be unaware that they have a dog, not to mention one that needs training—yet they came to you.

That leaves only 4½% that will be totally open, honest, effective and dedicated to training and providing or be able to provide the leadership and training that the dog needs without any help from you. Naturally, you'll rarely see such people—what do they need from you?!

10

What Happens During the Interview?

Hopefully, the client has filled out the form in such a way that checking back on the information recorded will be easy for you. And, if you decide to fill out the form for the client, you will be, in essence, doing the interview at the same time. Either way, it's what happens after the form is filled out that will enable you to get an idea of the interaction between the dog and owner. Perhaps a sample snipped from an interview would help:

The dog is a five year old female spayed Doberman, owned by a married couple in the 30's with no children. The initial H=husband, W=wife, and C=counselor.

Interview	Notes
W: We've been through murder with this dog . . .	"OK, let's check this together" indicates your desire to check what the client wrote and allow them to expand on it. Use the form to structure your interview. You continually review and clarify the information on the form by simply reading back to the client what they have written or said.
H: We're happy to be here with you to get to the bottom of these problems.	
C: Whoa—hold on a minute. I want to check back with you on some of the information you noted on your form, ok? Then	

Interview

we can get into the problem areas.

(Review of information on form continues)

C: Let's talk about some of the things you've mentioned about diet.

W: Alpo, two cans a day . . .

H: Is that good? We really don't know what to feed.

C: Well, for now, let's just collect some information and then I'll come in with the heavy criticism later—ok?

(all laugh)

(Later in interview)

C: When you took the dog to the obedience course, who went with the dog each week, let's talk about that.

H: I did because she wouldn't.

W: Couldn't is more like it. I can't handle her.

H: But you certainly know how to give her treats, baby her.

W: Well, honey . . .

H: C'mon, you know you baby her. You know you do.

W: OK, OK, I do, well, I suppose that's part of the problem . . .

pause (intentional)

Notes

Never let the client run away with the interview and don't attempt to discuss the "problem" first.

Check into major areas like lifestyle, diet, former training and people in the home with the dog, but don't criticize any major area at this point—wait until you've progressed through the entire form. Use humor to diffuse the situation if you suspect that you will have to criticize an area later.

When you get into the interview the flow of the interview itself will bring out certain problems. In this case the wife over-indulges the dog, gives the dog too many treats and generally "babies" the dog. But if the counselor were to make this observation it would have much less impact than if the couple is allowed to introduce

Interview

C: Well, don't look at me, you said it yourselves.

(general laughter)

(Later in interview)

W: . . . and that's the main problem, she's just WILD, crazy. She'll run through the house grabbing things, towels, toilet paper, whatever, and I can't catch her, ever.

C: How hard do you try? Do you chase her?

W: Oh, yes. I trip, I fall.

C: What's the dog do when you trip and fall?

W: She waits until I get up and then we go at it again.

C: Have you ever noticed a gleam in her eye at that point?

W: Oh, yes.

H: I've seen it too.

C: It's a game to the dog, a game you've taught the dog to play.

W&H: Yes, yes, it's a game at this point.

C: Let's see what we can do to stop the game. We can put a leash on the dog and just let her wear it for a week, dragging it around the house. We can do a lot of things to stop the immediate problem, but it might

Notes

it themselves. When you get a break like this, *shut up* and sit back. Let the participants explore it themselves, and again, use humor to diffuse the situation's tension, without, however, having the point lost in the joke.

During the interview the "presenting problem" comes out—in this case the client's opinion that the dog is hyperactive. It's a term commonly used to describe an active dog, but, in fact, very few dogs are clinically hyperactive. If you guide the interview the clients themselves come to the conclusion that the relationship is what is

Interview	Notes

Interview

not get any better unless we find out the ways that you cue the dog, even if unintentionally, that a chase is about to begin, that a chase game is even OK. After we find that out, we have to go a few feet deeper into your relationship, and then we can develop a program based on that.

W: I see, so stopping the chasing isn't the whole point.

H: No, what he's saying is that it will just come back again, maybe a new problem. We have to change the way we live with the dog.

Notes

riddled with problems—the "problems" themselves can be worked on, but the underlying cause has to be discovered and worked on too.

Once the interview is on chart, it handles itself, in a sense, and you can give information on how to stop immediate problems while always hearkening back to the basic philosophy that the relationship itself needs examining. However, it's often just not possible for a client to grasp any more than the basic tenet that something is wrong with their relationship with the dog. It may take them a few days after the interview to discover what that something is, although an amazing number of dog owners know what is out of sync when they enter the interview.

During this interview a five minute discussion erupted about the dog's past. The Dobe was a stray and had been procured via a friend of a friend. Without much factual information to go on, the wife had conjured up a terrible childhood for the dog—beatings, whippings, poor diet, etc. This led to an interesting but useless discussion of the dog's past—every minute detail of the dog's past, much of it unsubstantiated. Information about the past is valuable to you only if it helps you to understand the future and never valuable if it in any way "absolves" the client from responsibility.

Never let the past run away with an interview! Keep the discussion focused on the present behavior of dog owner and dog. If the client continually brings up the dog's past, blow it up by explaining clearly your philosophy of the "past." It is a common escape clause dog owners use in order to explain behavior they do not understand. Imprinting in early life *can* be a real trauma for many dogs, but dwelling on the dog's past really helps no one, wastes time that could be spent devising current solutions to current problems and makes the interview process a downbeat, wrenching affair that doesn't inspire hope and confidence in the dog owner.

11

Zingers

I AM INDEBTED to Don Arner, editor of *Off Lead,* for the term zingers. What are zingers? They are short, snappy, memorable sentences designed to impress clients with the urgency of training and that refer the client to proper sources of help.

Often in the veterinary office, boarding kennel, animal shelter or training office—with all the activity implicit in these settings—clients will confront us with behavior problems. We are well acquainted with the client who, on the way out the door states, "Oh, by the way, Ripper bit six people last week, what do I do?" You may not have the time or even the inclination to help the client at this point, but you can throw a good zinger their way and hope for the best.

During counseling itself, zingers are useful to re-direct an interview the way you want it to go, to jolt a client or to speed up the educational process. Always wait for a reaction after throwing out a zinger—for they are reactionary statements.

Here are some sample situations and sample zingers:

Complaints about canine aggression:
I'm very disturbed to hear about that kind of behavior, Mrs. _____ and I hope you seek out training right away. Situations like yours usually get worse, not better, unless you seek out training. Please call _____ as soon as you can to get help.

Complaints about house soiling:
You're talking as if you are this dog's maid. Unless you like it that way, you'd better consult _____.

Classic lines have great truth in them.

General bad behavior, especially aggression:
I think your dog feels responsible *for* you rather than *to* you. That's a heavy load for any dog to carry. The situation could become serious. Please call _____ for help immediately.

Guard dog advocates, people who want attack training:
I wouldn't suggest encouraging those traits in your dog. Do you have insurance that covers plastic surgery for children?

People who ask about shock collars as training aids:
Would you want an electrician to train your dog?

When you do not feel qualified (or interested enough, or have enough time) to counsel on a problem:
Animal behavior is of great interest to me but it is not my specialty. But I know someone for whom it is . . .

You must memorize zingers at first. Otherwise you will not have them in the back of your mind to deliver quickly at the right moment. All old-timers in dogs have a stock of zingers, and very few are original. It is a kind of oral tradition within the dog fancy—some statements just get handed down continually. One of the oldest is the RAF saying, "Every handler gets the dog he deserves" and even classic lines like "Let sleeping dogs lie" have great truth in them. Your work can be enhanced by good zingers, and the time you spend memorizing them and mentally cataloging them will be handsomely paid in educational impact and in laughs from your clients. Humor in counseling is essential, so essential it deserves a chapter of its own.

12

Criticism and
Humor

 Nobody, but nobody likes to be criti-
cized. Yet, dog owner counseling does include criticism of the dog
owner. There is no way around it: sooner or later the counselor will
have to say something critical to the dog owner. The key to effective
criticism lies in technique.

For instance, try to recall the last time you criticized someone.
Did you communicate your own irritation and anger over the
person's behavior? Did you say things that might shame the person
you were criticizing? Did you scream or lecture the person? Are you
even sure the other person understood the criticism and did you
check? Did you lord it over the person and claim your way is the only
way of doing something? If you answered yes to any of the above
questions, chances are, your criticism did not hit home.

For the dog owner counselor, criticism is something that is
given to the client, not inflicted on him. Complex levels of ego and
self-involvement link the owner to his or her dog. The dog is viewed,
often, as an extension of the self, and if the self is criticized so is the
dog, and vice versa. "Love me, love my dog" is still highly operable
and most owners, given the choice, *forced* to make the choice, would
prefer criticism of themselves to criticism of their dogs. Which is fine
by the dog owner counselor, for, in most instances, the dogs are
perfectly nice beings responding to the quirks of their owners.

To handle the delicate area of criticism, I usually say something
right at the beginning of the interview to the effect that, "I'm sure
you realize that I may have to criticize your handling of the dog in

some ways. I asked you about this on the form and you indicated that that was OK with you. I'll try to be as gentle as I can in the criticism, but I can't mince any words with you—after all, you're employing me to get to the bottom of the problem, and that might entail some criticism—what do you think?" Then, if I am working with the owner in a helping capacity in active training I will again state that I may have to criticize handling techniques: "OK, we're going to be doing some very active work. I might have to correct you about the way you're handling the dog. Sometimes I will have to give a correction very quickly, and 'please' and 'thank you' might have to go out the window for a little while. Timing is very important and I'll have to interject with criticisms just as you are performing something that's wrong—otherwise you won't be able to understand what you are doing that's off. But, I also want you to know that I will praise you exuberantly when you are on course—and I will mean that praise. Do you understand what I'm getting at?"

Whatever you say, say *something* about the fact that you will have to criticize. Don't just assume that the client understands that this is part of the process. In the same way, you should welcome self-criticism—explaining that if something isn't clear, you'd like to hear about it. Every dog owner counselor should have a follow-up evaluation form that is sent to clients after training and counseling have been completed. This form should ask the basic question, "Were you satisfied with the training you received?" and should be structured so that criticism is actually drawn out of the client after the working relationship is over. My form asks questions like, "Was the form you filled out clear and easy to read?" and "Did you understand the advice on nutrition and diet?" You can invite the clients to return the form unsigned, and some of the most helpful follow-up sheets I have received have been full of scathing criticisms, carefully typed out to conceal the identity of the irate owner! But it is the only way to learn how you are doing, not to mention how the dog and client are doing post-training.

One way around criticism is humor. The dog owner counselor must be funny. The dogs themselves provide enough humor, it might be said, but the counselor should strive to make interviews and training sessions as humorous as possible. One method is to employ "acting" in your sessions. I have no hesitancy to get up and "act out" a routine for my clients. I couldn't care less what they think of me.

For instance, it is one thing to describe how over-emotional hello and goodbye scenes can encourage chewing in dogs. It is another thing to get up and act out for the client exactly what you mean. I rise, go to a door and bend down, practically sobbing, stroking the bewildered dog. The client is sitting there watching and inevitably a grin of recognition comes over the face. I plead with the dog, "Please, Rascal, don't chew today, pleeeze, pleeeze, don't chew, I'll be right back, baby, in just eight hours, so don't chew, whatever you do pleeeze don't chew . . ." Then I leave. I come back in immediately and ask the client what they think the dog is feeling. They usually answer, "I think he's near emotional collapse," which is accurate. "Now, do you see why he might chew? I'll bet if you had a video camera trained on him and went down the hall to watch, he probably chews within a half hour of such a scene. Who wouldn't? The chewing comes from frustration, not anger—do you see?" In the same way, I'll get up and mimic the emotional "hello" scene that many owners re-enact night after night. I'll go outside, burst into the room, throw myself onto the floor and roll about with the dog, apologizing for being away so long. By this time the client is not only entertained, he or she has definitely learned something. They will regulate their comings and goings in the future so as not to put an emotional overload on the dog that may encourage chewing and other destructive behavior.

You can act out most anything for your clients and the time you will save in explanations is tremendous—it is one of the most effective techniques a dog owner counselor can employ, and the dogs will almost always go along with the act willingly. The client also likes the fact that you are working with the dog in this way, including the dog in the charade.

Cartoons, too, are great teaching aids and should not be overlooked. The hilarious dog cartoons of Carol Benjamin, which accompany this book and appear frequently in the *American Kennel Club Gazette* can be used to drive home points to clients. Watch the Peanuts strip carefully, for Snoopy gets himself into enough jams that sometimes very helpful cartoons appear—occasionally illustrating quite complex points of canine behavior. *The New Yorker* is a good source of dog cartoons, and the cartoons of Melissa Bartlett that accompany Jack Volhard's and Gail Fisher's *Training Your*

Dog, The Step by Step Manual (Howell Book House, 1983) are excellent—and educational.

Use any means possible to educate your clients, and make them laugh in the process. Blamers and placaters, especially, have to learn to laugh with, and even at their dogs, and especially at their own handling foibles. When the humor level goes up, the dog will sense it, and training will become easier, smoother. If only most owners had the sense of humor most dogs possess the world would indeed be a funny place to live. About every fifth dog I meet has a good sense of humor—jovial, self-entertaining, able to somehow get over the doldrums of the owner. The other four dogs would laugh more if their owners gave them the slightest indication that it was a good thing to do.

13
Over-Verbalization

"*Oh, GOOD GOD TIPPY, not this game
again—didn't we study the down stay in obedience class last week,
didn't we, didn't we? Now down, you heard what I said, down, it's
spelled D-O-W-N, recognize it? We learned it last week, and you did
it. Downnnn, pleeze, Oh boy, what a dog, C'mon, I said down, Oh
hell what's the use?*"

You can tell the over-verbal client a mile away—because you
can hear them. And when they come into view, you can tell from the
bored look on the dog's face. The dog tuned this owner out a long,
long time ago. In much the same way that the husband tunes out the
proverbial nagging wife, the dog simply doesn't relate anymore to
the wall of sound that is always audible. Since the owner is *always*
talking, it's impossible to hear what he or she actually has to say, and
the poor dog doesn't see any point in trying anymore.

The over-verbal client talks at the dog constantly, and obedience commands are mixed in with such a flow of words that the dog
cannot decipher them. Over-verbal owners often give contradictory
commands, the classic one is constantly saying "C'mon" and then
adding a command like "down." The dog is trying to figure out how
to come and lie down at one and the same time—quite a challenge,
and some dogs will then creep into their owners in a crouched
position hoping to satisfy both commands. Of course, the distraught
owner doesn't even know a contradictory command was given, and
just thinks the dog is being disobedient once again.

Over-verbalization is a malady that seems to affect urban
clients more than rural ones, for some reason. Perhaps it's the fact
that city dwellers often have to talk more in order to negotiate life in

the big city, or that verbal skill is more highly valued there than in the silent world of the country. Whatever the source, I've found that when I have a client from New York City or Boston, there is more of a chance of over-verbalization than from a country dweller. The hardest part is enlightening the client as to what they are doing to the dog.

It might be helpful to describe the silent lives of wolves to the owner, noting that these animals are the dog's ancestors. Except for an occasional group howl, these animals live in silence. You might also suggest that the client read the chapter "Silence and Your Dog" in *How to Be Your Dog's Best Friend* or the chapter entitled "Silence and Animals" in Max Picard's book, *The World of Silence.* Even if the client doesn't get the point, they will at least have to be quiet while they read these sections, and you may be spared telling them to their face that they talk too much.

Over-verbal owners are almost always placaters. They plead with the dog in strained, anxious tones. If you cannot get through by suggesting reading material, you might have to talk about the concept of over-verbalization in an abstract way, explaining that a dog must be able to hear and "section out" a command word in order to learn it—or obey it. If you still don't get through, you can take the dog and demonstrate, talking like the client does, having the dog not respond, and then descaling the rhetoric so that the dog does. Don't let the client misunderstand that correcting a problem with over-verbalization means not giving praise. Invariably, over-verbal owners are not praising their dogs but pleading with them. There's quite a difference. Yet, when you point out the problem some owners, probably as a self-defense reaction, will clam up completely and just go through the motions of training in much the same way the true computer type personality executes training. Whatever method you choose to explain the problem, it must be eliminated for very little progress can be made until the dog is really looking at and hearing the owner.

Over-verbalization often becomes a problem when the dog lives alone with just one person. The person may talk to the dog constantly. Studies show that as many as 35% of dog owners will talk to their dogs about how their day went, what they plan to have for dinner, even their love life—especially if they are alone with the dog. While this type of exchange might be therapeutic for the owner

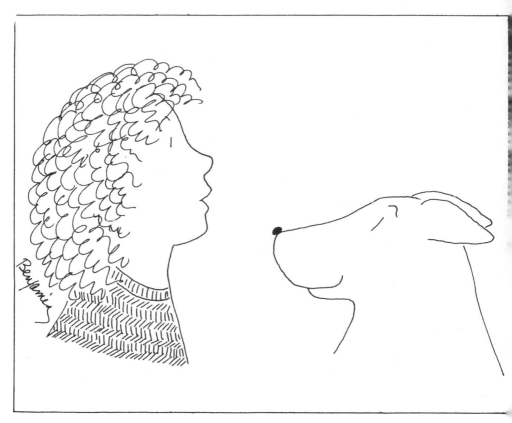

Many dog owners will talk to their dogs about how their day went, what they plan to have for dinner, even their love life . . .

and entertaining for the dog, it may be distinctly harmful for their overall relationship. Over-verbal owners with problem dogs must be instructed to shut up until the problems clear up.

A classic case of over-verbalization at work is the owner of an aggressive dog who strokes the pet and talks to it as the dog is growling, thus rewarding the behavior. This is over-verbalization as a form of unintentional training. The dog sees a stimuli, which could be as innocent as a leaf blowing past its face, or as serious as a real intruder, and immediately begins growling. The owner bends down, puts a hand in contact with the dog, begins stroking and/or fondling the dog and lets loose with a torrent of words. "Oh Missy, no, no, no, bad doggie, baaad dog. We musn't do that, no, no, no. It's all right, it's all right—it's okay, it's okay." The dog makes the interpretation that the owner is scared and worried—which, of course, the owner is. Only the owner is in most cases much more concerned about what the dog is going to do next than what the stimulus may be. But the dog has heard those worried tones before, and since no command words are mixed in (even "no" doesn't really register at this point—assuming the dog knows what it means anyway) the dog feels duty-bound to defend the distraught master or mistress, who, of course, is still running off at the mouth. Each time such a situation develops, which may be two or three times each day, the owner is unwittingly conducting an unintentional training session. And it is a *good* session, too! It has all the elements of a good training session: it has a beginning, middle and end, and it succeeds in teaching the dog something. I often wish clients could have *intentional* training sessions as neatly structured and highly developed as the unintentional ones they hold with their dogs day after day.

Over-verbalization in a dog owner, then, can be deadly. It can produce great confusion in the dog's mind and make it next to impossible for the dog to really listen to anyone. In the owner, over-verbalization is almost always a reaction to stress—often stress experienced because of the dog's behavior. It becomes a vicious cycle that the counselor must break for the client.

14

Teaching Specific
Techniques

THE PURPOSE of this book is not primarily to teach trainers how to instruct clients in the basic commands. There are other manuals for class instructors, notably Winifred Strickland's *Obedience Class Instruction for Dogs* (Macmillan, 1965) and other manuals that will teach you how to teach others to teach their dogs to come, sit, stay, down and heel. My purpose will be to talk about some techniques that are rarely covered in such texts and teach you how to impart them to your clients. Some of these techniques really demand a "live" demonstration, but I'll try to say what I can here.

Eye Contact

Wolves keep order in the pack primarily through eye contact. A piercing glance can stop a disagreement and a kind glance can denote acceptance. Eye contact is an essential element in the owner and dog covenant and hearkens back to a level of communication and understanding the dog craves. Unfortunately, most owners look at their dogs about as much as they look at other people, and most dogs look at their owners only when *they* want to—even if they appear to be riveted on the owner 99.9% of the time. There is a difference between the dog following the owner with its eyes in a casual way and the owner demanding eye contact from the dog. Because eye contact is often not present in the relationship, it must be introduced in a structured way.

76

Eye contact is an essential element in the owner and dog covenant and hearkens back to a level of communication and understanding the dog craves.

Tell the client to have at least two eye contact sessions with the dog each day. Sit the dog, tell the dog to stay, step around in front of the dog and animate the dog saying, "Watch me!" or other such phrases. Wait for a moment of good eye contact and sustain it for 3-5 seconds, no longer. This eye contact must be obtained quickly. The owner should be cautioned not to stand before the dog cavorting and jumping up and down in order to get its attention—or the eye contact sessions can become just one more way the dog tunes the owner out.

If the dog cannot yet hold a sit-stay, hold the dog in one by applying some light upward tension on the end of a lead. It may be possible to position the lead so that it helps to lift the dog's chin up to help the dog make eye contact. Other methods of getting immediate attention are to make a light stamping motion toward the dog, or use animated phrases like, "Psst, psst," or making clicking sounds with your mouth or snapping your fingers. Sometimes quarter-framing one eye with the thumb and index finger will help orient the dog's attention. When a few seconds of *sealed* eye contact have been obtained, during which the client's and dog's eyes are locked, end the session with light verbal praise. Stand behind the client so that you can read the dog's reaction and be able to tell when *sealed* eye contact has been made. Instruct the client in eye contact by first demonstrating with the dog yourself, then detailing the steps above.

The point of this structured approach is not ornamental. The client is trying to obtain eye contact on a somewhat artificial level at first, but soon the dog will begin looking at the owner more and more upon just the click of a finger or a phrase like, "Watch me, now." When the dog is giving the owner this off lead, and the owner anticipates giving a command, eye contact can first be solicited and then the command given. In other instances of problem behavior, the problem can be "warned away" by first getting eye contact and then delivering a warning phrase. The need for physical discipline then decreases and the relationship becomes centered on eye contact, denoting leadership on the part of the owner and responsibility on the part of the dog. Besides, it's fun!

Discipline

The discipline techniques described in *How to Be Your Dog's Best Friend* are the ones I teach clients, but a few words might be added here. First, these techniques must be demonstrated for the client as it is difficult for most owners to get a good idea of how to discipline from text and sketches. The Shakedown, Alpha-Wolf Roll Over and under-the-chin corrections all demand some sense of timing, and one technique may be better for some and another for others. Since many clients may not even be aware of proper discipline techniques, it is often best to give them reading material detailing the techniques (such as the monks' book) and then practice the techniques using a large pillow or other pliable object. The owner must be cautioned *not* to use discipline on dogs with severe behavior problems until he or she fully understands the application of such methods.

Remember, your job is to teach the client a new attitude toward the dog, not to diagnose every possible instance of bad behavior. If the client understands the principles of proper discipline, the application usually follows. Remember that discipline is swift and sure—brood bitches do not spend hours disciplining unruly puppies. The matter is disposed of in seconds with a firm shake or other reprimand. Once a client called me and said, "I read a book on disciplining my dog and I followed through on every technique. I took Butch out into the back yard and had it out with him for one hour." Chances are, the dog thought it was all a game. I'm glad the owner thought he accomplished something, but the truth is he probably didn't.

Long Down

What is called a "long down" in standard obedience classes and what is really needed in a long down are two different matters. Usually, five minute downs are taught, and the class instructor just hopes the dog will graciously expand the time of the down when at home. Trouble is, repeated five minute down-stays taught in the typical class become training sessions for short downs at home. The first thing owners of problem dogs need to teach the dog is a thirty minute down. Jack and Wendy Volhard emphasize this in their seminars and their reasoning is sound.

First, the long down is a way of showing dominance over the dog. Second, most owners can do something with thirty minutes whereas five minutes is next to useless. Third, there is much more of a chance that thirty minutes will extend to one hour or more by virtue of the fact that the dog may fall asleep than there is that the dog will voluntarily extend a five minute down to a half-hour down.

Many clients respond with shock and humor when asked to begin teaching their dogs a thirty minute down. The dog has never downed itself for three minutes on the owner's command, let alone thirty. You must explain that the thirty minute down does not include times during the day when the dog decides to lie down itself, nor does it include the time when the dog is asleep. A thirty minute down is imposed by the owner and, at least at first, carefully monitored by the owner.

The client should choose a time of day when practicing the down will not take time from any other essential activities. During television, reading or dinner is a good time to practice the down. At first, the client might have to interrupt these activities, eat with a chair cocked out away from the table and employ other measures in order to replace the dog into the down-stay if it moves. But the sacrifices are minimal for the great pay-back that will be coming. You must instruct the client to be absolutely rigid about enforcing the long down. If the dog finds it can test the owner on the down, the whole exercise may become another chance for the dog to be dominant.

Ideally, the dog has been taught the down and down stay in advance, and if this is not the case, work on it for at least one week before enforcing long downs. After that, have the dog hold at least one and even two thirty minute downs each day. Place the dog on the down *away* from the heart of the action in the room. Clients are often tempted to place the dog directly underfoot in the belief that this will make it easier for the dog to hold the down. In fact, it makes it harder, as the dog can easily misinterpret any movement on the part of the owner (getting up for the phone, or to turn channels, for instance) as permission to break the down stay. If the dog is placed on the periphery of the room, where there is little chance of having to move, and where the owner can make eye contact with the dog, there is more of a chance of a successful thirty minute down. While *brief* eye contact can be made, especially if the dog looks like it is getting up, the client should not stare at the dog. The dog will feel invited to get up or even compelled to come to the owner if the stare is prolonged. Nor should the client talk to the dog or even about the

If other pets are present in the household, they too should be on downs, except for cats and goldfish.

dog while the dog is on this down. Children in the household have to be instructed that the dog is on a long down and is not to be bothered. If other pets are present in the household, they too should be on downs (except for cats, and goldfish!) or sequestered elsewhere.

After a while, the dog begins to make its own decisions to lie down more frequently. After a few days of enforced downs, the owner can begin giving the verbal command, and will no longer have to physically take the dog to its place, place it on a down, move away and then monitor the dog out of the corner of an eye. The dog will instead enter a room, greet strangers and go into a down on its own. But in the early stages, if the dog gets up, the owner must be merciless. The owner should go immediately to the dog and place it back in exactly the same place, verbally reprimanding it. If the dog again breaks, discipline might be in order. If the dog continually tests the owner, something is wrong and you may have to do several down-stays with both yourself and the owner present.

Exercise

You wouldn't think you'd have to teach owners about the value of exercise, but the sad fact is most American dogs are over-fed and under-exercised. Many owners feel that good exercise consists of simply turning the dog loose for a run, or opening the front door and irresponsibly giving the dog free rein. Most dogs, given this kind of freedom will run for awhile, and then stop at every interesting smell along the way. A far better way to exercise the dog is to roadwork the dog on a leash by jogging with the dog. In this way, the dog is forced to keep moving, and the owner is too. Jogging on leash with the dog can become a form of communication between the owner and dog that can help to relieve behavior problems at home, especially those stemming from a neglectful relationship.

15

He Bites, My God, He Bites: (Counseling Concerning Aggression)

PHONE CALL: "Hello, is this the training school? It is? Good, wait! . . . Hold on. Oh no! He's coming at me—get him, Frank, grab him, oh no, shut the door, quick! Hello, are you still there? Listen, we need your help *badly* . . ."

While the above might sound like part of a rejected script from a bad TV sitcom, it will have a familiar ring to many dog owner counselors. While the antics of some owners as they attempt to cope with naughty dogs may be funny, aggression in dogs is no laughing matter. We can no longer minimize the problem: every year one million people are bitten by dogs. The Center for the Interaction of Animals and Society at the University of Pennsylvania, which offers a consultation service to dog owners, reports that aggression is far and away the most popular complaint. While obedience class instructors have all had dealings with aggressive dogs in their classes, for the dog owner counselor, meeting aggressive dogs may be a daily experience. Unfortunately, aggression is by far the most common and most important canine problem—and it is probably the least understood.

The first thing any counselor should be ready for is vivid descriptions of just how bad it can get. There is literally no end to what dog owners will put up with in terms of aggression from their pets, including personal injury—not once, but time and time again. A common reaction of many new to dog owner counseling is shocked incredulity when dog owners launch into terrifying descriptions of violent episodes they've experienced with their dogs. Typical situations: Patty F. had been bitten three times over three months when she attempted to remove the dog's feed pan for cleaning. Mr. and Mrs. Spitzler had to trick the dog into the garage each night using hunks of steak as bait because otherwise the dog would maul the husband when he attempted to get into bed with his wife. Mr. Conger hated coming home from work, because he knew "Tippy" would be waiting for him—usually hiding behind the front door, preparing to lunge.

One rule: don't try to hide your shock. Go ahead, act shocked—you are anyway. But don't act as if you don't believe it. You should, the client is probably telling you about half the terrible truth. Incredulity isn't of any use in your job—but honest shock and even disgust might go a long way. I've tried the route of the "cool professional" not reacting and remaining detached as Mrs. Smith displays the stitches they had sewn on her arm last week after Prince ripped it open. It doesn't work and it doesn't help the client. I've found that clients need to see shock, they need to see you react with concern *and* disappointment. They need to hear someone come out and say, "Why are you living like this—putting up with this?" Usually their neighbors, family, friends and sometimes even strangers have already stated this, but when the dog owner counselor says the same thing, it has impact. You must immediately remind them that they are not alone—aggression is a common problem. As soon as you've listened to the vivid descriptions, reacted sincerely and shown concern, you will have won the client's trust; you are suddenly in this problem together. Now you can tell the client how they may be to blame and what they can do to correct the behavior.

Types of Aggression

First, on the basis of the description of the behavior, you must label it. At the same time, you are trying to get an idea of the pattern of communication on the part of the owner—do they placate, blame, compute, distract? Aggressive behavior may fall under any of the following classifications or it may fall under several:

Fear-induced
Learned
Pain-induced
Territorial
Inter-species (dog fighting)
A response to teasing by children *or* adults
Genetically predisposed
Jealousy-related
The result of brain disorders (petite or grand mal seizures, biochemical, lesions, infections, etc.)
A response to medications
Focused on other animals (predation on chickens, cows, deer, etc.)

You can use the above listing or structure your own. Many find that simply making a series of check marks after each category helps them to get a handle on the problem and allows the client to keep talking. A great many counselors, even very experienced ones, simply cannot or will not trust their evaluations of aggression in a given dog on the basis of what the client says and insist on seeing the dog immediately. Even then, more than one meeting is often necessary just to label the aggression. It is too easy to label the aggression simply on the basis of what the client says, attempt a solution and find out later that it was wrong. My advice is to conduct the initial interview, meet the dog, begin perhaps some basic obedience work, and leave. Let the initial interview sit and simmer, and remove yourself from the dog's environment. Your head will clear, you will be less tense, you will relax and be able to think creatively about the case. Don't try to do it all in one day—even just labeling the aggression can take a long time. Explain that the treatment is going to take time. The dog didn't get that way in one day; it got that way over a long period of time with a lot of unintentional training, and you can't turn the whole situation around in one day. You need to say this to the client, and you need to say it to *yourself*. Take it slow.

I never try to set up a program for an aggressive dog until I have worked with the dog and its owner for at least one week. Obviously, such training cannot be done in a class setting. While class training may help owners of aggressive dogs gain mechanical control over their dogs, it often does not confront the underlying causes of the aggression. However, I must stress that *every* aggressive dog must learn the basic commands—sit, stay, come, down and the long down—before any treatment of the aggression problem takes place. In other words, do not try to discipline aggression in a four-year-old male Doberman—train the dog first to the basic commands.

Too many counselors, especially those with little interest or expertise in obedience training are attempting to treat aggression without providing the dog and owner with any structural building blocks such as come, sit, stay and especially down-stay. The distraught owner then tries to apply sometimes very sensitive techniques (sound therapies, shaping techniques, "flooding" and systematic desensitization are a few examples), without having any real training commands to fall back on. No type of therapy should be applied unless the dog is also being worked in obedience—for the dog must see the owner as the Alpha figure who asks for obedience and gets it. If the dog in question *does* have obedience commands under his belt, they must still be sharpened up, quickly. To put it in easily understandable terms, I usually try to get any aggressive dog to at least a 180 obedience score level in all of the basic CD exercises, except the ornamental "finish" exercise. I also begin to teach a long thirty minute down right away. I do this before treating the aggression and sometimes as I treat the aggression.

You may be saying, "OK, how do I train the dog before treating the aggression if he won't let me get next to him?" Good point—but there is a way—ask most class trainers, they know! Don't praise the dog with petting or bring your hand into close contact with the dog. Hold the leash up and out of the way and have the end coiled to bring over the dog's snout if the dog begins to act up. By "act up" I do *not* mean growl at you or attempt to bite you, I mean when the dog's eyes get hard, you correct him—watch for that certain hardness in the dog's eyes as you move about in training, but look over the dog to see it, not directly at the dog. Let the dog heel four feet away from you if that's what the dog wants to do. You can always reel the dog in later in another session. Use a lot of verbal praise and very little physical contact at first. If you really need to keep the dog away from you, string a lead through a piece of metal or plastic piping which you can use to push the dog away if he exhibits aggression. The main point is to get the dog out and get the dog *working*. Give the dog's mind something to think about besides biting you. This session should be very quick—even if the dog doesn't perform well, keep moving. Watch your movements, no jerky, strange motions, but do move along sprightly. This work makes a tremendous impact on most dogs and sets the stage for more specific corrections for the aggression problem later on.

This is not to exalt obedience training as a panacea for aggressive dogs. It is not, and this is shown by the fact that many aggressive dogs have already *had* basic obedience training. But is it tight? Is it reliable? And, most importantly, can the owner apply it? What is the owner's sense of *timing?* It's probably terrible. Yet, some behaviorists hand out remedies to clients such as sound therapies and other techniques that demand a fine sense of *timing,* the very talent that so many owners of aggressive dogs lack and had difficulty with in basic obedience work. If the owner cannot train the dog to heel because of a lack of coordination and timing (and this is perceived clearly by the dominant dog), what makes the behaviorist think he or she will be able to successfully apply, say, a sound therapy technique for aggression that requires an even *quicker* hand on the button or jingle of the sound therapy device?

Another point concerning your initial, fast-paced working session with the aggressive dog: some dogs will tolerate some obedience training and even appear to enjoy it—for ten minutes. Then, they've had enough and come at you. It's always a possibility, so make your first session short and end it on a happy note.

Taking the aggressive dog off its territory is another possibility in order to be able to begin basic obedience work. If you have a facility for boarding dogs, a week away from the owner and with you might do wonders. If you work in the home, be sure that you instruct the client to have the aggressive dog (for that matter *any* dog) *on leash* when you come to the home. It may then be possible to have

Give the dog's mind something to think about besides biting you.

the owner begin some training, on leash, and slip the lead to you. Another possibility is to take the dog for a walk and work in obedience someplace off its turf. If the problem is territorial aggression all of these approaches may help.

Digging for Information

Often counselors must dig, and dig hard for information from evasive clients. I've found that 50% of the clients with aggressive dogs are hiding a lot of information I need. They are not being evasive to make my job harder, but because they are ashamed of the problem they are having with their dog. They'll say things like, "Well the problem is, he just gets a little *uptight* sometimes." Translation: He bites if cornered, anytime, any place. "He's had a hard life, I'd be cranky too." Translation: an abused stray recently picked up by the owner and now biting. "Just leave her alone when she's eating and she'll be fine." Translation: If anyone gets within thirty feet of the dog's food or water when the dog is eating or drinking, the dog attacks. "He doesn't like men" (or women, or black people or white people or purple people). Translation: The dog is over-protective of its owner.

Another common scenario, so old it should have been set to music long ago:

Counselor: How many times has the dog bitten?
Wife: Once.
Husband: Three times.
Counselor: There seems to be a disagreement.
Wife: Two of those three bites were just nips.
Husband: Eleven stitches for one bite and three for another—you call those nips?
Wife: OK, OK, two bites.
Husband: He's got to have all the information, honey.
Wife: All right already, three bites!
Counselor: Three. Sure?
Husband: OK, all right, we'll level with you, *five* bites.
Counselor: Do I hear six?
Wife: No, really, five.
Counselor: Great—we only wasted five minutes on that. Now let's

get down to work. Tell me about each bite beginning with the first one—everything about each incident.

It's all understandable, and, after you've done this kind of work for awhile, eminently predictable. Remember, it's not a plus, in fact it's a distinct minus to own a biting dog in our society. The client is usually guilt-ridden over the behavior, does not want to admit it exists, knows it does, and is often terrified that the dog will turn on them next. They've often structured their *whole lives* around avoiding triggering the aggression. They know *exactly* what sets the dog off, including the speed the dog can be aroused. Everything is geared to avoiding this if at all possible. Just let the clients talk, and they explain how they live with the problem. A client I'll call Sarah gave me this description.

> Well, when I get up in the morning I have to get out of bed very carefully. Why? Well, I don't want to wake up King, because he'll growl at me if he doesn't get to sleep until at least eight-thirty. So I tiptoe to the bathroom and then get dressed quietly. I go downstairs and eat breakfast quickly because he'll be up any minute and it's impossible to keep food on the table when he's around—he just takes what he wants. I have to make sure the bathroom door is shut because he takes the end of the toilet paper and starts running around the house with it so that it wraps around everything. Also I have to have his food dish down and ready when he gets downstairs because he doesn't like me offering him his food. He doesn't like anyone near his dish. I have to watch the kids because if they let him out when they run for the bus there's no telling what he'd do to the kids at the bus stop. I let one kid out at a time and I throw a dog treat into the next room to distract King. He doesn't like to be brushed either, so usually there's a lot of vacuuming to be done. I rented a post office box rather than have the scene with the mailman every day, and I go to the drug store to get the daily paper—a fast trip, since King gets lonely easily and will rip up the house—rather than risk the life of that poor paperboy. He already got him once. So I've had to make a few adjustments to live with this dog.

If this client could hear herself, she'd see clearly that her life is now structured around avoiding upsetting King. She knows exactly what sets him off—she doesn't know why. When you hear such stories, you should be gleeful, for you are receiving very valuable information. You are looking at your most valuable asset in handling the problem—the client. The client has all the information you need in order to set the dog up to deal with the aggression. Let the client know how valuable this information is to you. You need it in order to help them to devise "set-ups" to correct the aggression.

Set-ups are essential in treating most behavior problems, and especially when working with aggression. You need to concoct, with the client, specific set-up situations to lead the dog into exhibiting the undesired behavior. You, in essence, elicit the bad behavior in order to correct it through discipline, diversion or some other technique. The crucial difference is that the client is now psychologically and physically prepared to discipline and control the dog's reactions. Set-ups have to be carefully explained to the client and sometimes it helps if the client writes the set-up scenario down and memorizes it, like so.

> Duke's problem is barking at the mailman. Every time the mailman drops off the mail (with Duke barking crazily inside) and then "runs away" it reinforces the bad behavior. My solution will be to do a "set-up" with the mailman. I'll talk to him and ask him to pause for a few moments after delivering the mail. I'll be ready—I know exactly when he comes. I'll be watching Duke carefully and immediately discipline him when he even *looks hard* at the mailman—not when he's in a never-never land of crazed barking. I'll have a tab lead on him to be sure he can't get away from me. I'll attach a warning phrase of "OK, Duke, don't even think of it," said in my lowest, most dramatic voice and after a while he'll connect the fact that discipline follows that warning tone of voice if whatever is being done (or thought about!) doesn't cease immediately. I'll beat this problem and have a happier dog when it's over. If I have any questions, I'll check with my trainer.

When a client concocts a set-up like that and has the dedication to map it all out in black and white, you've made real progress. You now have a structure. The client is no longer placating the dog or blaming it—they are doing something creative to stop the undesired behavior.

For More Information

This book will certainly help you to help clients with aggressive dogs, but further study and experience will be necessary. For more information concerning specific techniques for dealing with aggression, the following books might be of help: *Behavior Problems in Dogs,* by William Campbell, especially the section pertaining to the "Jolly Routine"—a diversionary tactic that can be employed successfully with many aggressive dogs; *Dog Problems,* by Carol Lea Benjamin, which contains a variety of observations and sure-fire techniques for treating aggression; *How to Be Your Dog's Best Friend,* by the Monks of New Skete, which contains a chapter on discipline techniques and one specifically on aggression; and *Help, This Animal Is Driving Me Crazy,* by Daniel Tortora.

General Obedience Training

▼

Specific Psychotherapy

▼

High Protein Dietary Therapy

▼

Chemotherapy

    Tranquilization

▼ **Antiandrogens**

Surgical Treatment

    Castration

    Tooth Extraction

▼ **Lobotomy**

Euthanasia
Progressive therapies for aggression.

From: Kirk Current Veterinary Therapy VI Small Animal Practice. "Clinical Behavior Problems: Aggression" by Katherine Houpt VMD, Page 872.

Progressive Therapies for Aggression

After reading these popular books you should begin to study the research done on aggression done within the veterinary community. The writings of Virginia Voith, DVM, Benjamin Hart, DVM, and Thomas Wolski, DVM, will be of great interest. Dr. Voith, who has worked extensively with aggressive dogs has published a copyrighted *Outline for Diagnosis and Treatment of Behavior Problems in Dogs and Cats* that is an invaluable aid for counselors (Victoria Lea Voith, DVM, Dept. of Clinical Studies, School of Veterinary Medicine, University of Pennsylvania). Dr. Katherine Houpt's short article in the 1982 *Kirk Veterinary Manual* should also be consulted as should past canine behavior columns by Dr. Benjamin Hart in *Canine Practice* magazine. These are now available in book form from the magazine. To learn more about aggressive behavior in dogs you must:

1) Read about it.
2) Work around aggressive dogs.
3) Work closely with those who train aggressive dogs.

This is one area of dog owner counseling where only hard, cold experience will be of ultimate benefit. Ask to work with trainers who deal with aggressive dogs. Observe only at first—watch the dog's body language, the actions of the trainer. Observe and memorize. If you are working with an aggressive dog under an experienced trainer's guidance, listen to what the trainer tells you to do quickly and without argument. This work can be dangerous.

Remember, too, that there is nothing wrong with saying you do not treat aggressive dogs. As one counselor said, "I'll train for obedience, for show, and I'll counsel for house soiling, chewing, digging, you name it, but I don't like getting bitten and I'm not interested in working with aggressive dogs." A hard lesson for many trainers is that they are not the only resource available and cannot handle every canine problem with equal expertise.

If you don't want to handle aggression cases, develop a referral system with someone who does. If you do, get ready—for at some point, you are going to get bitten. Never, ever work with an aggressive dog alone. Be sure someone is around to help you if you need help. Please do not discount the possibility of real danger from aggressive dogs, regardless of what you think your abilities are. If you are doing this kind of work, *please* always have an assistant near.

Watch the dog's body language.

People often ask me how I handle working with aggressive dogs on an interior level. They ask if I feel afraid. Of course I do! It's terrifying to take the end of the leash with a dog on the other end who has a colorful biting history. But someone has to do it, and the alternatives are pretty grim. And, such progress can be made. It's so beautiful to see an aggressive dog change its mind about life, stop feeling threatened by every leaf that blows by and begin to enjoy life. It's rewarding to literally save a dog's life and inspiring to see owners relax and live securely once more. You just have to psyche yourself to do it, and you have to tell yourself that you won't be afraid—even though, of course, you will be. But not as much after you've told yourself you won't be!

I often think about Ashley Montague's statement that aggression is just inverted love. He meant it for humans, but perhaps there is a point there for dogs, too. Inside the aggressive dog is a wonderful dog ready to be brought out.

Finally, when I meet an aggressive dog I think of the example of St. Francis, who tamed the wild wolf of Gubbio, and of Daniel in the lions' den who must have used diplomatic and yet forceful body language to keep the lion's jaws shut. Did you know that the phrase, "Do not be afraid" appears 366 times in the Bible? That's one for every day of the year and an extra one for leap year! Think of that the next time you meet a growling dog.

16

He Chews, My God, He Chews: (Counseling Concerning Destructive Behavior)

AFTER AGGRESSION, complaints about destructive behavior will be the most frequent wails of despair the dog owner counselor hears. And wail the clients do. Unless you've been there, you can't imagine the pain of coming home to a house completely stripped of expensive draperies, molding, even precious art works. So *don't* think counseling such clients is as simple as saying, "Pick up everything off the floor you don't want destroyed," because many dogs can *climb*. If they can't climb they might hurdle or leap, anything to get to whatever object is targeted for destruction.

Advice that should be right at the top of your list is instructing the clients on how to regulate emotional homecomings and departures. The concept of *acting this out* was explained in an earlier chapter. The client should greet and say goodbye to the pet quietly, and affectionately, but calmly. The owner should not try to sneak out of the house, but rather call the dog, sit the dog and make eye contact with the dog, explaining to the dog in a few brief sentences that he or she is leaving—and trying, by the tonality of the voice to instill a sense of responsibility in the dog. A special toy can be kept nearby, and the owner should scent this toy by rubbing it between the palms or putting saliva on it. This toy, a durable one, is then thrown dramatically just as the owner leaves. The dog will be distracted by the toss and will locate the scented, "personalized" toy later when frustration builds and chewing urges mount.

A consistent program must be set up with the owner leaving the house on fake errands for only 5-10 minutes. On the following days, the "errand" is stretched to fifteen minutes, then twenty and so on. Each time the dog manages to stay alone for even a few minutes, it is a big victory. Nothing encourages like success, and the dog will build on small successes. Owners of chewers must immediately *stop pleading* with the dog not to chew, especially when they leave home. This pleading is usually anxiety-ridden, worried placating, worrisome to canine ears and obnoxious to human ears. You should *act out* for the client exactly what type of pleading you mean. Adopt a whining, nasal tone, turn up the end of each sentence and demonstrate for the client, "Pleeze, Queenie, pleeze don't chew—I beg of you, while I'm gone pleeze don't chew. . ." Never act out poor handling methods in an attempt to humiliate the owner—do your acting out in a humorous way with an eye to educating the client.

Many clients who own chewers rev their dogs up into a frenzy upon returning home, hoping to "wear out" their own guilt feelings over having left the pet alone. The burden of this neurotic homecoming scene falls squarely on the dog and comes out in chewing. Be sure to explain how worried vocalizations upon homecoming or departure instill anxiety and fear in dogs, and that this later erupts into frustration-release chewing. (Usually right after the client closes the door in the poor dog's face or comes home to open it with a wild hello scene.)

In counseling for destructive behavior, the owner must be placed firmly in the dog's paws. Here, some "anthropomorphic" counseling might be acceptable; "How would you like to be alone for eight hours with nothing except forbidden items to chew on?" The

The dog will locate the scented, "personalized" toy later when frustration builds and chewing urges mount.

owner must be made to see what it's like from the dog's point of view. Above all, you must explode the myth that dogs chew to "get back" at their masters. Dogs are morally neutral. They don't think about getting back at someone but they do get frustrated, and some individuals get frustrated quite quickly and quite easily.

Discipline for Chewing

Physical discipline for chewing is not always effective, but some swear by it. Clients should be taught humane discipline techniques, but only if these techniques are seen as exceptions to the dog's normal training. Discipline methods like taping the chewed object in the dog's mouth, chasing the dog around the house with the object, hitting the dog over the head with the chewed object or dangling the chewed object from the dog's collar are useless, and in the first instance, dangerous techniques. Envision an ineffective, unsure owner who is viewed as submissive by the dog, attempting to tape a slipper into the mouth of a strong, dominant German Shepherd dog—a dog that already knows a considerable amount about the power of its mouth. Yet, such discipline techniques are still routinely handed out. As William Campbell notes: "Unfortunately, practices which should have been outlawed along with medieval tortures persist in many 'modern' obedience books and neighborhood training programs." As a counselor, you should not put a client in the position of having administered discipline and having it backfire and worsen the relationship with the dog.

For this reason, be especially careful about recommending discipline for chewing after the fact. If the owner storms into the house, grabs the dog and shakes it—three hours after the dog has chewed the draperies—the dog will simply associate the owner's coming home with getting walloped, and will become tenser as the terrible moment arrives each day, and will chew more. Some clients will already have gotten themselves into terrifically tight binds because of this misuse of discipline. They must be started back at base one. All discipline for chewing, unless it is administered just as the dog *begins* to mouth a forbidden object (and then only a verbal reprimand should be necessary), should be eliminated. A wire crate can be employed to buy the owner and dog some more time and to break the vicious cycle that has developed.

A wire crate can be employed to buy the owner and dog some more time and to break the vicious cycle that has developed.

If the chewing is in its very early stages (not more than two or three episodes), it *may* be possible to use discipline after the fact *if* you are sure you can make an association in the dog's psyche. Taking the dog to the scene of the destruction and administering the "Shakedown" correction as described in *How to Be Your Dog's Best Friend,* will be the episode that most dogs need to eliminate chewing, but later methods must also be taken. It is a good idea to try to make the discipline look like it is coming from the *environment* rather than from the owner. This can be done, for instance, by strategically setting mousetraps around the area the dog frequents for destructive behavior, using repellents or arranging furniture so that it will fall if the dog goes near that area. Chairs and small tables can be easily placed for such a set up, but don't rig a dining room table or a chest of drawers for such a crash!

You must design time-charts for your clients to be sure that they are structuring their "fake errands" correctly. The owner must be cautioned not to goldbrick on this problem. Because one fake errand is successfully negotiated by the dog does not mean that the dog is over the destructive behavior hump. The complete program of fake leave-takings must be run through until the dog is going the time necessary for the owner. Obviously, if the owner wants to leave the dog alone for an extraordinary stretch, you have to warn the owner that this isn't a reasonable goal. An excellent pamphlet is *The Lonely Dog, Victimizer or Victim?* which was issued by The American Humane Association (5351 S. Roslyn Street, Englewood, CO, 80111). It is well written, and hard hitting. In a short text, it explains that dogs are dogs, not people, and that owners should examine their motivations for getting a dog along with taking a look at whether they are really willing to put in the time and effort required to meet the *dog's* needs.

Remember to teach the client to approach the problem positively, also. They should provide a substitute toy *and* adequate exercise before they leave. There must be a daily play session, preferably not immediately upon arrival home, but at some point during the day. All tug-of-war type games must be immediately eliminated, for in these games the owner can unwittingly be encouraging chewing and is putting himself, often, in a submissive position when the object being tugged is released and the dog "wins." The dog's diet and general lifestyle must be fully reviewed. It's

If the owner wants to leave the dog alone for an extraordinary stretch, you have to warn him that this isn't a reasonable goal.

Something else is usually wrong in the relationship between owner and dog.

usually a good idea to suggest suspension of any and all food treats for at least three weeks, or until the chewing is cleared up.

Finally, something that should be obvious—chewing is not an isolated problem in dogs. Something else is usually wrong in the relationship between owner and dog. If this underlying problem is not detected and changed, the chewing might be the least of the owner's concerns one or two years down the line. Aggressive behavior, self-mutilation, chase and nip behavior and invariably some form of unpleasant oral behavior may be waiting in the wings. Is the relationship permissive, placating? Is the dog neglected? What is the overall tenor of the relationship between the dog and owner?

I always tell whining owners of chewers to be grateful—the dog could be biting them. They should also be grateful that they have finally come to the point of doing something about the problem, and conscientiously resolve to follow training instructions to the letter, instead of trying to interpret "why" the dog "hates" them so much.

For every client who comes in to me with a sob story about destructive behavior, I have an even worse sob story to relate to them. Our job as trainers and counselors is always the same: we help clients to stop moaning and complaining, we help to eliminate feelings of helplessness and we set them to work on training. Instill hope in your clients. Once I had a client who had the edge of a Chagall painting gnawed by a canine beaver. The painting was mounted six feet off the floor, over the bar. The dog had mounted the bar to get to the painting, knocking over a bottle of Chivas Regal and fine Russian vodka in the process. Fortunately, only the frame was chewed and a couple of threads of the canvas dislodged. This was my most critical case, for the owner was irate, guilty, yet determined to do *something* in "revenge." The woman was referred to me by her veterinarian, who called me early that morning and asked me to convince the woman to see me. She had driven her dog to the veterinarian and left orders to have the poor mutt executed at high noon. I won the dog a reprieve through a feverish counseling session, and subsequent training sessions. The dog now admires all of the precious art works in the home, from floor level.

17

Problem Behavior and Nutrition

IF A DOG is experiencing behavior problems , you must advise the owner on the dog's diet. You have little choice, for if you do not collect information about the dog's diet and counsel the owner concerning it, you will be ignoring an important factor in the dog's life. When someone describes the dog's diet by saying, "He eats three cans of canned dog food in the morning and a bag of Soft n' Chewy at noon, then he has a bowl of Sugar Smacks, his favorite cereal, and a Big Mac at night," you really owe it to the client to say *something* and you don't have to be a nutritionist or a veterinarian to comment.

Remember, we can eat what we want when we want to eat it, assuming we have the kind of food we want around. Except for canine thieves, our dogs get what we give them. Some owners feel, "Well, since he can't get the same variety of food as I can, I'll at least leave the food down all day so he can have as *much* as he wants." This practice works well with some dogs and leads to obesity in many. Free-feeding can also be the root of a housesoiling problem, and if this is suspected, immediately advise the owner to schedule two feedings a day.

When to Feed

In my experience, the vast majority of dog owners feed their pets once a day around 5:30 p.m. The fact that the dog's stomach is empty all day doesn't seem to dawn on many owners who feed "when work is over" simply because that is a convenient time for them, and even for reasons as vague as, "That's when my mother did it with the family dogs."

When, as an adolescent the dog begins to refuse to eat on a frequent basis, the owner usually begins once a day feeding, supplemented in many cases by treats during the day. But the dog may need two meals in order to alleviate hunger tension. Frequently dogs with oral problems like pica, chewing and stealing food can be helped simply by feeding an *early* morning and an *early* afternoon meal. This insures that food will remain in the dog's stomach all during the day. A *light* treat can then be added just before the dog retires to escort the dog's stomach through the night. Contrary to a popular belief, it is not true that a dog will sleep better on a full stomach.

Different dogs metabolize nutrients at different rates, and more active dogs may "burn off" their food at a faster rate—especially if they are self-entertaining and on their feet most of the day investigating, probing their environment and generally active.

Variety

It is destructive to the dog's intestinal flora to constantly switch feeds, but many owners do, to alleviate diet boredom they perceive as bothering the dog. These owners are probably the most difficult to get through to, simply because they have already sold themselves on the importance of a constantly changing diet. You must carefully explain that the dog's intestine cannot take this kind of variety, and far from doing good, such a diet can lead to irreparable harm. For some, the motive is economical. "I buy whatever is on sale," is a common response, but the savings in dog food will later be added to the veterinary bill.

Caution the owner to make the changeover to your preferred food gradually, adding not more than 25% of the new ration at any one time. Further caution the client to follow your instructions to the letter and not to experiment.

Collecting Diet Information

If you wish to counsel concerning canine nutrition you must have the knowledge with which to do so, and you must find out

106

The dog may need two meals in order to alleviate hunger tension.

exactly what goes into an individual dog's stomach during the course of a 24 hour day. In other words, you must find out what makes up the daily feedings, what type of treats are given, how often, by whom, and also explore whether the dog has supplementary sources of food. These sources may not be known to the owner and could consist of tipping over neighborhood garbage cans, killing rabbits and other small game, being fed by the neighbors or other covert sources. Check out brand names, and write everything down. Don't depend on the client to give you all of the information you need on the interview form, as they will inevitably forget the 4:00 p.m. mini-meal they have gotten into the habit of feeding lately. "Oh, that's not a *real* meal," will be the response. But the dog eats it, doesn't he? If there are children in the family, you must check out what they feed the dog, for it could be the dog is being fed correctly by the owner with the children giving treats out of their lunch boxes also.

Method of Feeding

Many dogs eat in a Grand Central Station type of atmosphere, their ration placed down while the rest of the family struts around the kitchen or children run in and out past the eating dog. Incidents of aggression often result when the dog perceives such stimulation as intrusions and decides to protect the food. Naive children sometimes tease the dog while it eats or attempt to remove the food bowl. For instance, children sometimes think it is funny to hear a dog growl, and a perfect way to agitate the dog is to pretend to remove the food bowl as the dog is eating. The dog lifts its lip and gives a low warning growl, but the child continues to reach for the bowl and is bitten. Amazingly enough, some adults think that they should be allowed to remove the dog's feeding pan at whim, even if the dog has not finished the ration, to show who is boss and some otherwise respectable training texts even suggest this as a method of showing "dominance over the dog." The whole idea, in reality, is an insult to the dog, who should at least be left alone to eat its food in peace.

Regardless of the current method of feeding, and especially if any behavior problems are present, I usually suggest that the food be placed down in a room, the dog put in the room for ten minutes, and the door closed. The owner should then return and pick up the food,

108

reoffering whatever is not consumed during that meal. The owner should let the dog out of the room used for the feeding, again close the door, and then pick up the feed pan, exiting with it. Under no circumstances should the dog be fed in the center of action in the home nor should any tug-of-war develop concerning the feed pan.

Type of Food

It's outside the scope of this book to discuss particular brand names. The pet food industry is constantly changing and new feeds are being introduced all the time. In general, I usually suggest that problem dogs be taken off any kind of food high in carbohydrates and low in protein. I try to put the dog on a ration that ups the protein to 25%-35% and lowers the carbohydrate intake to the middle teens. Inevitably, this means removing the dog from the typical commercial foods and placing the dog on one of the "alternative" dry foods. For the most part, these foods are made in smaller batches and shipped from one plant to distributors and then on to dealers, who then sell them to the public privately. Invariably they are not available in the local supermarket. If you suggest such foods, it is important that you have on hand all of the necessary information concerning locations for purchasing the food and nutritional breakdowns of the products. Because the public recognition factor for some of these foods is much lower than it is for commercial foods backed by large advertising campaigns, you may have to spend some time explaining how they were developed, tested and are distributed. One difficulty I have found is because these foods are less well known, clients are often very hesitant to use them. The media and the dog food industry have done quite a job on people's minds, and unless they have seen the product advertised on television, they sometimes don't believe it exists. This lack of consciousness can be alleviated by procuring from the company materials describing the foods. Several companies publish attractive brochures explaining the history of the company and the background of the foods.

Needless to say, you must be conversant with these materials and able to articulate why you suggest one food over another. You must be ready for the ever-present reply, "My veterinarian said to feed Tippy Brand X," and realize that many veterinarians are not skilled nutritionists and will tend to suggest commercial products with a high recognition factor that are easy for the client to obtain. Without appearing to contradict the veterinarian you can suggest that the client check on the new diet with the veterinarian for his or her approval. Far from being miffed, I've found most veterinarians appreciate the fact that someone knowledgeable finally sat down with a client to map out a reasoned diet. Before suggesting any radical diet changes, be sure to check the animal's health history.

Additives

The research involving hyperkinetic children and their diets is well known today and may be applicable to dog diets. While not enough scientific experiments have been done to say anything conclusive, we do know that many dyes and other additives can have harmful effects on at least some dogs. Removing these from the dog's diet by serving foods with lower traces of additives, or by feeding a strictly natural diet is to be suggested as a hedge against high excitability and problem behavior.

Vitamin B

William Campbell, in his nutritional studies involving dogs, suggests the supplement of a B Complex vitamin formula to the diet to take care of any possible thiamin or niacin deficiencies that may be connected with poorly conditioned reflex formation or hyperactivity. He wisely calls the addition of a B Complex vitamin, "good behavioral insurance." My work with problem dogs seems to bear this out, although I have never been able to control enough factors in how the dog is fed and pilled in order to do a longitudinal study of the matter.

Sometimes it is difficult for clients to find a vitamin B supplement formulated for dogs, so a human supplement can be suggested. Emphasize that the vitamin *may* have a calming without a tranquilizing effect on the dog, and that this is a course of vitamin therapy, not drug therapy. You will find that clients who use vitamins as a family and know first hand the good effects stemming from such use will be quick to understand your rationale. Families with poor nutritional habits often feed their dogs poorly, too.

Treats

Because the majority of problem dogs perceive themselves as the Alpha figure in the home and are used to getting what they want when they want it, one of the first courses of action is to cut off the dog's supply of treats. Often in giving treats, the owner places himself or herself in a subordinate position vis-à-vis the dog. If they produce the treat box, and without asking the dog to do anything, bend down and give the treat quickly, the dog could be reading the body language and overall interaction as submission on the part of the owner.

Some owners treat so often that the dog is kept in a state of near-constant agitation hoping that a treat will come its way. This then leads to overt moves on the part of the dog to con the owner into giving more and more treats. Half the time the dog is not even really hungry, and may even leave the treat on the floor, but simply enjoys re-establishing its dominant role in the household. Since it is impossible to change many clients' perception that giving food treats is the same as giving love, you must simply forbid them to give any treats whatsoever until the dog's behavior is exactly what they want it to be—and what you want it to be. Don't try to cut these clients down to one or two treats a day, as they will continue to give ten—down from twenty a day, but still far too many.

18

Grooming

THERE ARE TWO ASPECTS of grooming I would like to talk about. First, what you look like, and secondly what the dog looks like.

When you see clients you should be dressed informally but neatly. Few clients expect you to be wearing a suit or tailored two-piece since you will be working with the dog, but you should be dressed nicely. Remember that black pants will pick up dog hair and show it, and certain fabrics, like polyester, seem to attract dog hair and hold it. Shoes with excellent traction are important. Charm bracelets, slacks with extremely large flairs and other items of clothing or jewelry that would hinder training should be avoided. Men with beards should have them neatly trimmed, not only to make a good impression on your clients, but because many dogs find a long beard fascinating and will attach themselves to it if it is long enough.

Grooming is important for the dog too. I always insist on a full grooming if I have the slightest feeling that the dog is at all uncomfortable because of matting, tangles or lack of a bath. I have seen, for instance, dogs with aggressive responses quiet down considerably after a complete grooming, which sometimes involves a full clip-down. Check for mats in the dog's hindquarters, and if you feel *any,* instruct the owner to have the dog groomed. If you want to know how it feels to the dog to live with a bottomful of matts, take a swatch of your own hair and put a rubber band around the base. Tighten the rubber band and leave it in place all day. By the time the day is over you will have a headache in that spot. Is it any wonder that aggression sometimes decreases when a full grooming is done?

I also routinely clip back the hair of any dogs with too much of it covering their eyes. Because I stress eye contact so much, I need to be able to see the dog's eyes, and I want the dog to be able to see mine. Some owners of Old English Sheepdogs, for instance, have never seen their dog's eyes, unless the wind blows the hair momentarily away from the dog's eyes. They are missing out on a vital link with their dogs. One owner told me, a week after we clipped back the facial hair on her Yorkie, "I love those eyes—and she's like a whole new dog to me."

If you take a dog in for training for a considerable length of time, it's standard courtesy to bathe the dog before sending the dog home. This, too, can be a form of training and I have had calls from clients whose sole training wish is for me to teach their dog how to stay in the bathtub during the bath.

19

Euthanization:
The Hardest Topic

W HEN AND WHY should a dog be euthanized? Is euthanization indicated simply because the dog is experiencing difficulties adapting to the human environment, and a counselor is baffled? For that matter, is it indicated because two, three or more specialists are baffled? The question of euthanization is a deeply ethical question, full of moral overtones and colored by a variety of emotions, opinions and dictums. Along with abortion, birth control, dying without "aids" and other weightier matters concerning human life, a question like this is in the limelight. Is there a distinction between animal and human life? As we come to know more about animals, is that distinction changing? All of these moral and philosophical questions lie beyond the scope of this practical book—yet they intrigue me as I'm sure they intrigue you.

Anyone working with dogs and their owners must come to a decision in terms of exactly where euthanization "ranks" in their list of alternatives for troubled dogs. Counselors who simply refuse to look at this matter at all, and may proclaim, "I have *never* advised euthanization," may reflect on the fact that it is not the specialist who indicates euthanization, but the client.

The counselor is only present as an advisor, his or her role is to indicate all the possible alternatives. It does not necessarily follow that a trainer indicates that a dog should be "put under" (a nicely elusive phrase) because he or she notes it in passing, any more than it means a priest condones abortion because he notes that it is an alternative to a pregnancy. For instance, I often indicate to distressed owners that I feel they have three solutions to *any* problem they may be experiencing with the dog:

1) Train the dog and live happily ever after.
2) Give the dog to someone else, who will probably have the same set of problems.
3) Euthanize the dog.

I spell out these alternatives for even minor problems if I feel a lack of dedication to confronting the problem on the part of the dog owner. These are the only alternatives for dog owners I am aware of. I feel explaining these three options helps to indicate the absolute necessity of *doing something* about the problem. Of course I indicate that the third alternative is a desperate one, one that most owners don't even want to think about—but still, I've set off the problem in bold relief.

The only instance, in my opinion, when it is acceptable for a counselor to directly indicate euthanization is the case of an elderly or infirm animal that is suffering, and another specialist (usually a veterinarian) indicates that the situation will not get better. I'd add, too, that most veterinarians, except in the most obvious cases, consult colleagues for affirmation of their decisions. My reflections here, however, do not focus on euthanization as a response to extreme health difficulties but as a "solution" to problem behavior.

Specialists who have counseled dog owners and trained dogs for years sometimes get a feeling for just which animals are not able to be rehabilitated. Obviously the extreme fear biters and genetic freaks are easy to spot. The dog that is totally out of control, lunging at the end of its leash, trying to bite anyone within reach, the dog that jumps in the cradle and mauls the baby, or the dog that has persistently and erratically bitten humans—even after corrective training—these are often cases where there is little or no hope, and no choice but euthanization.

Still, even with this over-riding intuition the counselor must check his or her feelings. You are not there to *tell* the owner what to do with the dog. You are present to listen, and if necessary, to guide the dog owner to an acceptance of the pet's death.

I once knew a trainer who believed in being "direct." He had received most of his canine training in the military, and had seen many dogs euthanized simply because they did not work well enough or had outlived their practical use. He had come to look upon euthanization as a fact of life. However, when he tried to transfer this "direct" mode of thought to the American domestic scene, he ran into difficulties. He told one client about her fear biter, "I'd put that dog under pronto," and the owner, shocked, frustrated, and feeling hopeless, did just that. Later I heard that other trainers had thought the dog was coming along nicely and making progress. However, regardless of the impact of this "professional" advice in my opinion the owner may have gotten off easy, for, if the dog really should have been euthanized, it was the trainer's responsibility to educate the client so that the same sad situation does not develop again. All of the blame was placed on the dog, and despite the pain of euthanizing the pet, it can be an easier route than realizing that part of the animal's problems had to do with your poor handling techniques. This trainer, who believed he was being honest and direct, actually circumvented the main issue: he denied the client the opportunity to see, through the prism of his experience and knowledge of dogs, exactly where the main handling errors were committed so that she could first gain the conviction and confidence to humanely euthanize the present pet, *and,* most importantly, gain the courage and confidence to learn from her mistakes and be able to do better with a new dog.

As it is, the trainer offered no hope, no solace, no real alternatives or education. He failed both the dog and the owner. Yet, how many times are even the most sensitive and humane trainers driven to frustration and find themselves saying (if only to co-workers) that a given dog should be eliminated. It's a well known fact, borne out in the research done by Elisabeth Kubler-Ross and others, that those who work in the face of death almost daily, whether it be human or animal death, often develop an unconscious insensitivity to those who die or those concerned with the death. As counselors, we must always be on guard against this, we must examine this area frequently, looking at the motives of owners carefully—and at our own motivations. Life, after all, is our goal, not death. We give in to death only as a last resort.

116

Are There "Bad Dogs"?

The thesis of the incredibly popular book by Barbara Wood-house, *No Bad Dogs,* seems to be that truly disturbed dogs do not exist. But this isn't true. In *Understanding Your Dog,* Dr. Michael Fox has an excellent section detailing the phenomenon of "psycho-pathic" dogs. Such animals do exist. Sometimes physiological factors are at work, and neurological maladies can be present. Occasionally, the underlying condition cannot be detected by the trainer or by a veterinarian, or even a team of veterinarians—even with the dog under close observation. Genetic aggression, especially in St. Bernards, German Shepherd Dogs and some other breeds is on the rise and very little can be done to rehabilitate these dogs. Something should definitely be done to rehabilitate those who breed such specimens, but often they have already gone out of business as soon as the genetic junk they flood the market with has matured into prime biting age. There *are* bad dogs, so to speak, but anthro-pomorphic thinking also has to be avoided. The dog itself did not choose to be "bad" and in almost every case, there is an unthinking or just plain stupid human who is ultimately responsible for the situation.

Some Source Materials

To find out more about how to counsel dog owners concerning euthanasia, visit your local shelter and strike up a conversation with almost any worker there. These are the sociologists of the dog world and they deal with the problem daily. One of their most painful tasks is the grueling one of deciding who lives and who dies when space becomes an insoluble problem. Frequently, the choices must be made along the lines of age, health and behavior. If the shelter is overloaded, aggressive dogs may have to be euthanized. Shelter personnel are also often presented with aggressive dogs that the owners *want* "put to sleep" although many shelter workers will refer such persons to trainers or veterinarians. "The first thing I try to determine," said one shelter worker, "is what type of training has the dog had to date, and does the owner want to continue?"

Most veterinarians will also be willing to share with you their feelings on the subject and how they handle it. I've spoken with

There *are* bad dogs.

many veterinarians who have developed excellent methods of relaying to a client the fact that euthanization is in order and can handle the task quickly, yet with sensitivity and tact.

Recently a text appeared that is bound to be of considerable help in this area. It is *Interrelations Between People and Pets,* by Bruce Fogle, D.V.M. (Charles Thomas, Publisher, Springfield, Illinois, 1981). Dr. Fogle, besides editing this fine volume, also contributed one of its best essays, "Attachment, Euthanasia, Grieving," in which he states, "Any discussion of euthanasia of pets must be based on an understanding of the attachment that develops between owners and pets." Later he adds, "The emotional strain (of euthanizing a pet) can be so great that 15% of pet owners when asked whether they would get another pet after the present one died said they would not because of the psychological trauma that followed the present pet's death."

Dr. Fogle also has some practical suggestions. He notes that very often people cope very well during the actual process of having the dog euthanized, in much the same way that some people can conduct themselves with great restraint during a funeral. But it is when they return home to the empty food dish, the leash, basket-bed and cupboard full of uneaten dog food that they crumble. "The following day, I write a note to the owners reassuring them that the decision they made was correct, humane, and most importantly, unselfish," Dr. Fogle says. This is a good practice for counselors involved in such cases, too. I usually add in the note that the step was in the best interests of the dog, that the owner *did* have X number of months or years with the pet, and that it is not the end of the world. If we have attempted training and have not been able to avoid euthanization, rather than viewing the training as a "waste" or a "failure" I mention that the owner can at least comfort himself or herself with the fact that they sought out the best training they could, when they could.

Don't suggest getting another dog—that is the client's choice, and might better be stalled for at least one month. *Do* suggest, tactfully, that *if* they decide to get another pet, after a waiting period, that they come to see you for help in selecting a new dog. Always end such sessions gracefully by adding that you are willing to be of any help, at any time. *Don't* say, "I know exactly what you're going through" (you don't) and *don't* say, "It's all right, everything will be OK" (it isn't and you know it).

Most of all, don't be surprised at the grief experienced by dog owners as they come to the decision to euthanize. Tears are a frequent reaction and actually a good sign. Even if, because of years in dogs, you are somewhat immune to becoming emotionally involved with every dog's death, any uncaring attitude will be immediately picked up by your client and decoded on the level of arrogance and lack of sensitivity. You should not coddle a client whose dog must die, but you shouldn't just tell them to have a stiff upper lip, either. Take the time to care.

One of the most sensitive pieces I've read concerning the death of a dog was penned by Carol Benjamin in the *American Kennel Club Gazette* (March 1983). In "No Way to Say Goodbye," she confronts the paradox "When your best friend dies, how do you say goodbye?" I'll close our discussion with excerpts from this beautifully touching tribute to her dog, "Oliver."

> One moment you're a have. An absent heartbeat later, you're a have not. For the rest of your life, or so it may seem, you replay moments on your internal screen. You reassure yourself by remembering good moments. You think about the first time you took him down to the river and the way he got "plugged in" when he saw his first duck. You recall those long walks right after the first snow, winter after winter. You can still see his face the way it looked when you brought the bitch puppy home, as much for him as for you. You think about running together, pacing each other, protecting each other, about doing shows at schools and making children laugh, about doing shows at nursing homes and crying all the way home. You can even feel the warmth of that broad head in your hand, as if he had come to say good night just one last time.
>
> You make yourself miserable, too, by remembering failures—always yours, never his. You should have taken him out more, for longer walks. You should have played more games. You should have taken him swimming more often. Maybe you shouldn't have gotten another dog. Even though he seemed delighted, maybe he was jealous and too big of heart to show it. And worst of all, you should have been there, your cheek resting on his paw, you should have been there when he died. You should have thanked him for all he gave you. You should have said good-bye.

Then, later on, she concludes,

> How do you say good-bye when, even now, time won't dull the image of those kind, brown eyes, those patient eyes, those wise and loving eyes. When your special dog goes and leaves you full of tears and love, there simply is no way to say good-bye.

120

20

Children and

Counseling

$\mathbf{W}$HAT IS THE ROLE of children in dog owner counseling? Let's begin by saying that children have a significant contribution to make in helping you understand the owner/dog relationship. You should include children in some of your counseling sessions. Listen to them. Children are often capable of shedding light on the interaction between the dog and the rest of the family. Many times in my sessions children have piped up with spontaneous comments that were very revealing—and helpful. Like the little girl who answered, "Because daddy kicked her," when I asked why the family's Cocker Spaniel was limping. Or the little boy who replied. "All over the house," when I asked where the family's Poodle defecated.

Age Stages

Age stage has a lot to do with what a child can offer to a counseling session. Let's take a quick look at how children relate to dogs. Very young children, pre-two years of age, are simply not aware of the dog as a real presence, although they may know its name and even talk to the dog. They will often relate to stuffed dogs in the same way, and with even more affection. After age two and up to age seven, many children view the dog as a funny thing that competes with them for parental attention. They may also see the dog as a friend (and the dog, in turn sees them as a littermate), but they won't hesitate to turn against the dog if it is perceived as taking time and attention away from them. At this age there is a lot of tail yanking, ear pulling and sometimes sexual stimulation of the dog. The child simply cannot understand being told *no* to any of these activities, especially if the dog seems to tolerate them. Parental supervision is a must. Parents must carefully monitor all of the activities between children and the dog. Play sessions between the dog and children must be watched. Play sessions that involve large groups of yelling, screaming, cavorting children must not include the dog. The danger that a child will fall down and begin screaming, triggering an aggressive response in a sound dog must not be overlooked. If the child is petting the dog in a wrong area, or if the child is being too rough with the dog, just saying *no* is not enough and will not educate the child in the proper way to have physical contact with the pet. Instead, the owner must drop everything and go to the child, showing the child exactly what type of contact *is* acceptable.

After age seven, the child enters the "concrete" stage. The child still cannot deal with abstract concepts, such as the "why" of a long down-stay, but the child will understand its necessity if he or she *sees* it demonstrated. Demonstrating obedience exercises is very important for children between the ages of seven and eleven. To them, seeing *is* believing. Complex discussions of the dog's behavior and the whys and hows of training will go right over their heads. But they will be very willing to cooperate on a concrete level. Children between the ages of seven and eleven often make excellent trainers. They will be very consistent in remembering sessions, will be firm during them, and will remember to include a play session afterwards. Occasionally if the pet is a member of one of the large, working breeds, the child may be afraid of the pet's size. But even this difficulty can be overcome using the following techniques.

The trainer has to start the child out on the right foot. Often, inserting the child, holding the leash in loose hands, between you and the dog is a good way to demonstrate the exercises with a dog who has had some work. Tell the child to do and say whatever you do or say. It's like the old "Simple-Simon" game. Then proceed through all of the exercises with the child sandwiched between you and the dog. The child should not hold the leash tightly, so that you can funnel corrections through to the dog. If the dog is just too active and wild, switch the child to the end of the leash with yourself in the

Children between the ages of seven and eleven often make excellent dog trainers.

middle, and then move the child back to the middle when things calm down. Just the presence of the child holding the leash near the dog has a great effect on the dog. This can be the beginning of a change in the relationship between the dog and child from one in which the dog sees the child as a littermate and playmate to be bossed around to one in which the child is viewed as an Alpha figure with at least some authority. Some children will literally scream the commands, in rapid sequence, and you must stop them if they do. Others will shyly mouth the commands. Don't proceed with the work until the dog is registering on the kid's commands and yours.

An excellent text for incorporating children into the training process is Carol Lea Benjamin's, *Dog Training for Kids* (Howell Book House, 1976) and a good text explaining early training practices is *Superpuppy, How to Raise and Train the Best Possible Dog for You,* by Jill and Manus Pinkwater (Seabury, 1977).

Children at this age need other responsibilities vis-à-vis the dog. They can take care of feeding the dog (under supervision) and washing the dog's food and water dishes. If they can't handle actual training, they can be employed as training distractions during down and sit-stays. This is a role most children will relish, but be sure they are not teasing the dog to break a stay. Some children will mimic the dog and hold a down-stay themselves—an added convenience for the owner!

After age eleven, children often develop interests of their own that do not include the dog. They may spend more time in after-school activities or with friends. The dog may grow listless during this period and may begin to vibrate toward the adult figures in the home. The dog may miss the play sessions that once were a featured part of every day, usually announced with the arrival of the school bus. The adults may have to provide a play outlet for the dog at this point. Still, even if the adolescent seems to act as though his formerly close canine buddy isn't any longer there, the two may occasionally go off for a walk and a "talk" together, especially if the adolescent is under stress. This type of warm contact is one of the truer aspects of the relationship between a dog and young boy portrayed on shows like "Lassie." When in distress, the adolescent goes off with the dog—the one family member who has never thwarted him, the one who understood him when he was a little boy and always gave unconditional love. It's in sessions like these that the years of hard work that go into owning a dog pay off—for the dog educates the child in the value of like virtues, the stability provided by loyalty, the support of friendship.

When you conduct the initial interview, try to get an idea of the ages of all the children in the family. Ascertain if anyone who was close to the dog has now gone away to college, or is rarely at home anymore.

Before they are seven years of age, children need not attend interview sessions. In fact they often scream and howl so much it may be better if they are left at home. If you work in the client's home, try to indicate that your initial session must be conducted minus phone, kids, household chores or other distractions. But after training begins, children, other than the very young, should be included in all phases of training and *see* it all.

William Campbell has noted, "Once parents become aware of their contribution towards a dog behavior problem, things are normally brought under control within a few days to several weeks, depending on the severity of the problem. However, if the parents involved do not represent effective authority figures with their children, rehabilitation is often difficult and prolonged, many times indicating qualified parent/child guidance as well as canine behavioral guidance."

21

How You Can Work Counseling into the Class Setting

WHEN A SECTION OF THIS BOOK ran as a series in *Off Lead* magazine I received a letter saying, "The series is inspiring, but I teach regular obedience classes, and I can't stop the class and sit down with everyone who is having a chewing problem with their dog. How can I offer some counseling in a class setting?"

First, any instructor should realize by now that counseling is going to mean more *time* with class participants. Unless you are willing to offer your students more time, don't offer any form of counseling. If the standard heel, sit, stay, down, stand, finish routine is all you feel you can conscientiously teach, do that and leave counseling to others. Develop a referral system so that the people with problem behavior or other concerns can get the time they need. If you *do* decide to integrate counseling into your class work, here are some ideas of how you can go about it.

Identify the Problems

Identify the problems in your class by using some sort of interview form, perhaps just the problem check-list shown on the forms in the appropriate chapter in this book. Study these carefully and group the students experiencing similar problems. For instance, owners of chewers can be notified of a separate meeting that will examine this problem and map out solutions for it. Owners experiencing problems housetraining their dogs can be lectured another night. Hand-outs and book suggestions can be given out and readings assigned. It might be best to keep these groups small, three or four participants, so that each owner gets at least some individual time.

If an owner has indicated on the form that a great many problems are present, such as aggression coupled with chewing or digging, it might be good to schedule a separate interview for this person. The interview can be conducted before, or after class but never during class. This should be made very clear at the outset. Students should know that if a counseling service is offered, it does not give them a free ticket to prattle on about their dog's behavioral problems during the class itself. Besides being time-consuming and boring for other students, these monologues break the flow of the class. Most good class instructors try to keep their classes *moving*— which is good for the handlers and dogs. But counseling necessarily means slowing down and stopping to listen, and cannot be done effectively within a class.

If you offer such a service as an adjunct to the class, be sure you dictate your terms. If separate appointments are necessary, give notice of the times that are convenient for *you*. If the student really wants help, he or she will make the time. Charging an additional fee is only reasonable if the counseling is going to take up valuable time. Advice on fees and the effect they have on a dog owner's mentality will be discussed in Chapter 24.

Offering a counseling service early in the class is also a good way of weeding problem dogs out of the class. I have heard stories of trainers who were bitten or even mauled during the first class by aggressive dogs which really didn't belong in a class (and, in most cases, were promptly dismissed). An owner may enter a class with an aggressive dog but decides to "wing it"—hoping the class routine will somehow work on the dog and stem the aggression, and so the owner just doesn't say anything about it, especially if not asked. Then the trainer gets bitten. But the trainer could have checked. Besides the real danger to life and limb, the owners of such creatures often become completely frustrated upon expulsion from class and euthanize the dog. All of this unnecessary anguish could have been avoided if the instructor took the time to ask more questions at the outset of the class.

The complaint that handlers will not reveal their dog's problems if they fear expulsion from the class is nullified if a counseling service is offered. We must realize that the majority of handlers, except for those enrolled in quite specialized courses, do not come into a training class in order to prepare their dogs for a CD title or in order to master technical handling skills or ornamental exercises. They come because the behavior of their dogs is not what they want it to be and they sense they might be doing something wrong. Even if we collect our fees, graduate our dogs, educate the handlers in some technical skills and dish out a few folk remedies to behavior problems, it will all be to no avail if the dogs go home and still jump up, bite, chew, dig, soil the house, act bossy and generally control the household. What have we accomplished?

This realization is dawning on a great many trainers who have been teaching standard obedience classes for years, but who now are offering some form of counseling within the typical class structure. Such courses become known very quickly, and draw more students than courses without counseling. Some class trainers are even adding nutritional counseling as part of the course. All over the country, new approaches are being developed that expand and enrich the structure of class instruction.

My records show that 25% of the dogs I've seen over twelve years, often dogs with severe behavior problems, have already been through a program of class instruction. In many cases the dogs were exceptionally smart and mastered the work quickly. Their technical work is tight—they can come, sit, stay, stand and down on a *dime*. Yet the underlying problems of aggression, chewing and so on were not dealt with in the class. While it's true that standard class training in and of itself can often help eliminate problems associated with lack of leadership on the part of the owner, it doesn't for all dogs, let alone all owners. The need for counseling in class is obviously there. It's our challenge to find innovative ways of integrating counseling into the class structure.

22

The Breeder

Becomes a

Counselor

In COUNSELING prospective puppy owners, individuals who have no vested interest as counselors may find themselves saddled with the task. Any reputable breeder, whether he or she breeds an occasional litter or on a larger scale, should realize the necessity for interviewing and counseling prospective clients. Literature spread by humane groups and other sources encourages people who want puppies to seek out good breeders who will inquire extensively about their needs and desires in a dog. An increasingly sophisticated dog-seeking public will demand this kind of attention from the breeders. It might as well be done right.

It is not only breeders who are involved in helping people pick puppies—often trainers and veterinarians are turned to for advice, not to mention animal shelter workers. It is challenging enough to help someone pick a specific breed, not to mention a specific puppy from a litter.

A German Shepherd Dog breeder, for instance, should not automatically assume that every client who comes to the kennel is suited by temperament and personality to own a German Shepherd Dog. Not everyone can handle every breed. The selection task might appear easier for a Golden Retriever breeder, but every breed has idiosyncracies that new owners must be aware of. Only the breeder or the experienced counselor has an intimate knowledge of given bloodlines.

Passing and Failing Clients

It might seem a simple task to separate good and bad clients for puppy ownership. But the task is not that easy. As noted, there is the problem of specific breed preferences and expectations, and the reality of what the owner can really handle. Careful interview techniques and forms should help you to "expose" unworthy clients. Here are several instances when a client should "flunk."

1) If the client gives any indication that he or she would abuse or neglect the animal.

2) If the client has a history of euthanizing dogs for behavioral reasons.

3) If the client is wavering about specific breed selection, or shows a complete ignorance of breed traits ("All dogs are alike, aren't they?" or "A Golden Retriever or a German Shepherd, it doesn't matter to me, they're both alike").

4) If the client has a physical handicap that would prevent proper care of the dog. This does not exclude all handicapped owners.

5) If the client is buying the dog for another party, and you have not met the other party.

One of the first questions you should ask, if you are, say, a breeder of German Shepherd Dogs, is not "Why do you want a dog?" but "Why do you want a German Shepherd Dog?" This query may surprise your clients, and they may remark that they admire the physical attributes of the breed, that their mother had one, or that they had one and it died. It is not snobbish to say that these are not necessarily valid reasons for selecting a given breed. When asking this question the counselor should look for an answer that denotes some kind of perception, on the part of the client, into the particular nature of the breed in question. For instance, a reply of, "I want a German Shepherd Dog because I admire their intelligence and because I had one before and know how to handle one," may be a rare answer, but even variations on this theme may denote a sensitivity to the particular temperament of Shepherds. With many of the large, working breeds, clients often answer in terms of the services they expect from the dog ("I want him to protect my family"). Common answers for prefering one breed to another may also involve status, ego and the owner's need for love. The counselor should be wary of any answers that highlight the services the dog is to perform for the "master." The owner/dog relationship may be off to a bad start.

Clients who reveal that they had a pet of the same breed (or another breed for that matter) and had the dog euthanized should be asked to explain the situation. If the death was recent, the person may find it difficult to talk about, and you should be sensitive to this fact. However, an answer is needed, since you have to know if the former dog died of old age, disease or was euthanized for behavior reasons. If the latter is the case, a more complete line of questioning must follow that focuses on this event, and that hopefully reveals important facts about the owner's environment, perceptions of dogs in general, and especially of the breed in question. You must tactfully collect information about the life style of the former pet, in order to advise the client correctly.

Once I interviewed a middle-aged man who revealed that he had owned three German Shepherds previously to coming to seek a new one. The first was a companion for twelve years, until old age claimed his life. "He was aggressive," the client stated, "but I learned to live with it." Dog number two lived five years and had to be euthanized because it suffered from hip dysplasia. This dog also had a history of biting. The third dog, recently deceased, also had hip problems. In all three cases the owner purchased a dog without a guarantee against dysplasia, via newspaper ads, simply in order to "have a dog." Something in the owner's personality or needs allowed the aggression to get out of control in his dogs. He appeared disinterested in seeking out a dog with a guarantee of hips and temperament. He talked freely about the demise of each pet.

It's important to act interested in such stories because it is often by listening to such vignettes that a client's handling skills (or, in this case, lack of skills) come to the fore. These stories may be utterly boring and even inane to you if you are anxious to place a puppy or move on to more interesting material. To many professional dog helpers, there is nothing more boring than listening to stories about dead dogs that one has never met and, obviously, will never meet. However, these stories are important as they often reveal the nature of the rapport between handler and dog.

In the above case, I declined to place a Shepherd pup with the client. Instead, I turned the interview around and made it into a breed-selection interview, which is where any fruitful prospective puppy client interview should begin anyway. By the time that client left, he was going to wait a month before getting any other dog, read four books I suggested, come and see me again, and was seriously thinking of a Labrador Retriever. The responsible breeder owes it to the client to conduct a breed-selection interview even if the client hasn't asked for it. Some clients assume they have decided on a breed that is "for them" when in fact they haven't gone about it intelligently at all. And if a breeder assumes that interviewing clients is basically to insure placement of his or her pups, they are also misinformed. Placement is nice if it happens, and of course it usually does, but an improper placement will simply result in an older, unruly puppy returned to your doorstep a few months later when the client, who was not interviewed correctly, claims they "can't handle it."

If you are a breeder and feel you must "flunk" a client, you should let them know your reasons for refusing to place one of your pups in their care. You're not very brave if you cop out and tell the client that you are suddenly out of puppies, or by referring the client to another kennel of the same breed who may be less inquisitive about their clients. If you think they should not have a dog, say so. If you think they would not do well with a dog of your breed, say so. Many clients will appreciate your frankness and may come back a few months later with a course of self-education under their belts, ready to give a wonderful home to one of your pups. Their reaction, of course, depends greatly on how well you handle the talk. If you need to suggest some general breed-selection books, my favorite is *Roger Caras' Dog Book,* which contains basically sane and balanced descriptions of the major breeds, including descriptions of potential faults of temperament, or Daniel Tortora's *The Right Dog for You: Choosing a Breed that Matches Your Personality, Family and Life-style.*

132

Introducing the Puppy

A wise breeder will not conduct an interview with a client with the puppy present, whether it is the puppy planned for the client or a random "sample" puppy. The client will pay too much attention to the puppy, and not enough attention to the answers they must give you. Because getting a puppy is a highly emotional and joyful experience, especially the first time the owner sees and actually holds the pup, it is best to forestall this emotional moment so that it can be savored after the more rational process of interviewing is over.

But many otherwise intelligent breeders feel that the clients deserve to see "the goods" and will give in to even the slightest agitation on the part of the prospective buyer to go and get a puppy, any puppy. Some breeders show whole litters to clients instead of testing and placing the puppies themselves—a far wiser approach. "Puppies sell themselves," one breeder stated sassily, "and this interviewing business is for the birds." This breeder spends hours on the phone fighting off frustrated clients who want to return her pups. The wise breeder is concerned not so much with *selling* puppies as with *placing* puppies in good homes. No adoption agency trots out prospective adoptees in front of potential parents before carefully interviewing the couple. If they did, the agency would be faulted for a "meat market" approach to placing children, and probably be closed down. The same approach should be censored in placing puppies. Accepting a puppy into one's home is in many ways just as difficult a task as integrating an adopted child into a family.

Assuming that a careful interview has been conducted and the client cleared, the puppy can be brought into the room. The room should be enclosed so that the puppy cannot escape, run down a hall, jump out a window (it has happened) or otherwise freak out. Shyer, less self-assured puppies should be carried into the room and placed in the new owner's arms, and, in fact, this is the way many old-time breeders like to conduct the first meeting. One breeder explained, "I teach the new owner how to hold his or her arms and explain to them that I will bring the pup in and place it with them. You have to show them how you want the puppy held in advance, otherwise they panic and may drop the pup. Placing the pup right in their arms avoids tense situations like the pup running away, which the owner might interpret as rejection when it's just puppy stress. The owner feels like a million dollars because even the shyest pup will begin to relate with a person who is holding it, licking the owner's face and so on. Everybody is happy, everybody wins this way."

New owners like to feel that besides picking the puppy, the puppy also "picked them" and a happy first meeting helps them in this not totally unreasonable hope. Thus the puppy that immediately runs up to the client who is an emotional push-over, jumping up, clawing, scaling the gleeful client can be seen as having "picked" the client. But this may be the worst puppy for that client— despite the illusion of total devotion and acceptance. All breeders and dog owner counselors should be fully schooled in puppy testing procedures.

A great body of work has been done over the last ten years on this essential evaluative tool. Five basic puppy tests can be found in Campbell's *Behavior Problems in Dogs,* and Melissa Bartlett's article, "A Novice Looks at Puppy Aptitude Testing" in the March 1979 *AKC Gazette* remains one of the best short expositions on the subject, including a sample score sheet for "grading" puppies. Acquaint yourself with puppy testing materials and do some puppy testing yourself regardless of whether you are a breeder, trainer, veterinarian or animal shelter worker.

To conclude this section, let me list some of the questions I'd ask on an interview form for prospective puppy clients. You should then add more of your own, including questions concerning your specific breed:

Basic data, name, age, number in family, etc.
How were you referred to us?
Are you interested in a puppy or older dog?
What are your ideas on pigmentation?
Why are you interested in obtaining a dog of our breed?
What qualities do you like in a dog of our breed?
What qualities do you dislike in a dog of our breed?
Is this your first dog of this breed? If no, explain.
Are animals now present in the home?
Have you examined the sales policy that comes with this dog?
Have you ever had to euthanize a dog?
Are you willing to spay/neuter this dog, and if not, why not?
Where will the dog stay during the day? At night?

Do you live in an urban, suburban or rural environment?
Have you read any books on dog care and training? If so, list them.
Tell us a little more on the reverse of what your needs and desires are in a dog.

23

Counselors and Veterinarians: Working Together

WHEN I BEGAN COUNSELING dog owners at New Skete, the concept was relatively new. In an attempt to explain the approach and how it differed from the usual class type of training, I developed a short presentation. During this half-hour session I explained the basic tenets of dog owner counseling and how it can be used as an aid in veterinary practice. I then made appointments with area veterinarians and visited as many as I could.

The response was tremendous. At that time *How to Be Your Dog's Best Friend* had not been published, so the doctors were responding to something other than media hype. First the veterinarians were grateful that I had called and made an appointment and that I had indicated in advance how much time I would need. They mentioned that other trainers often just dropped in, often at the worst possible moment. Secondly, they were impressed with the professionalism of the approach as they went over the forms being used, the type of records I kept and became acquainted with the overall format of dog owner counseling.

The presentations were not high-powered nor geared to selling the concept. I simply presented the idea, explaining that I was available *if* the doctor wished to work with me on a referral basis. A packet of business cards was left behind with the receptionist (it's a little tacky to hand them directly to the veterinarian). The stress was on the help I wished to offer the veterinarian and his or her clients, not on what the veterinarian could do for *me*. Finally, I indicated on the phone that I would be as brief as possible, and when I was actually talking with the veterinarian, I was as brief as possible. Veterinarians are busy people.

Each practitioner was approached with the knowledge that they are often turned to for help with canine behavior problems. But it was added, tactfully, that perhaps they felt they lacked the time or expertise to help in such matters. It should be noted that because of the pressures of veterinary study, most students receive only a minimal grounding in animal behavior, unless they decide to specialize in that area. From yearly seminars I taught to students from Cornell University, I know the extreme stress these students are under to master an immense body of knowledge in a short period of time. Add to this the fact that entrance into veterinary school was, for many, an uphill battle from which they have barely recovered by the time studies begin. Somewhere along the line, something has to give. "I'd say the two areas that we miss out on—not completely, but substantially—are behavior and nutrition," one third year student told me at a seminar. "Yet, these are the very areas we will be questioned about frequently in practice."

A third area that often suffers is that of professional relations. The veterinarian, besides setting up his or her own practice, complete with expensive equipment, must also be a financial wizard, a public relations person and a kind of liaison between the veterinary community and the others involved with animal work. Unfortunately many veterinarians do not, at the present, view trainers, breeders and other animal workers as fellow professionals involved in animal care. Often a hierarchal model exists, with veterinarians on the top of the ladder and others several rungs below. While veterinarians may have something to learn in this area, it is also true that all too often trainers and breeders do not act like professionals and shouldn't be surprised when they are not treated as such.

"Acting professional" does not mean having a degree or swank office or an appointments secretary. Nor does professionalism mean snobbism. On a concrete level professionalism means attending to the following:

1) Keeping careful records of work you do with clients.

2) Working responsibly on a referral basis with others, including sharing records, providing copies for files, consultations.

3) Outside of consulting with others in the field, keeping dealings with clients confidential, even if the subject is "just a dog."

4) Being always willing to learn from another person in the field, remaining open and willing to re-think old thoughts.

5) Attending seminars, clinics and workshops that pertain to our field and keeping up to date on new developments by reading trade and professional journals.

Working with veterinarians can be a joyful and rewarding experience. So many behavioral conditions overlap with general health conditions. For instance, aggression can often be connected with hip dysplasia, panosteitis and spinal problems. Only an x-ray and consultation with a veterinarian will help you to understand these conditions. Grand mal and petit mal seizures often have serious behavioral effects. The epileptic or narcoleptic dog often suffers behaviorally. These are just a few of the areas where the skill of the veterinarian and the dog owner counselor overlap.

Drugs like Ovaban are now frequently used in controlling a host of behavior problems in dogs and cats, especially aggression in dogs. Often the veterinarian does not have time to explain the action of the drug on the dog, and the importance of concurrent training. The dog owner counselor can be of great help in such instances. One veterinarian put it this way, "Ovaban (megestrol acetate) can be of great help in some behavior problems, but whenever I prescribe it, I also prescribe a trainer, if the client hasn't already got one. There's much more chance my drug regimen will work if I also have the help of a competent trainer."

It's often comforting for your clients to realize that you are willing to work with their veterinarian. "Who is your veterinarian?" is a question you should certainly ask on any behavior case history form you develop. If the client does not have one, make a referral and stress the importance of general health checks, and of forming a working relationship with a veterinarian before any serious problems develop, not after. If you are not a veterinarian, you can aid the doctor by stressing general health check-ups, parvo virus shots, correct inoculations and all the other areas and medical concerns that owners tend to overlook. If you are a veterinarian you can stress the vital importance of early training, behavioral control and working on behavioral problems before they hit a crisis point. You can add a counseling service to your practice, by employing a full or part time consultant or by making referrals. You can stress to your clients that you feel you have a moral responsibility to treat the *whole* dog, and that besides being able to take care of their clinical and surgical needs, you are able to be of help concerning the dog's behavior.

Another benefit of working with veterinarians is the seriousness with which their clients take what they say. Clients view the veterinarian with deep respect. If he or she refers them to you, they are that much more likely to really listen to your advice. By the same token, if a breeder or trainer with wonderfully healthy dogs frequents a given veterinarian, it can be an indication of the respect the breeder or trainer has for that practitioner.

One more point: Don't refer to veterinarians as "vets," unless they specifically indicate that they don't mind. It rankles some who feel they did not spend years in veterinary school to be referred to constantly with a slang term. Most of us would not call a human doctor "Doc" or a psychiatrist "shrink," at least not to his or her face, yet the term "vet" is common parlance.

Finally, veterinarians should recognize the fact that responsible trainers and breeders may be an endangered species. For the betterment of dogs, we should begin to work together on a more intense level. Training organizations like the National Association of Dog Obedience Instructors and local clubs might develop more of an outreach to the veterinary community, and professional organizations like the American Society of Veterinary Ethology might open up their ranks to more qualified trainers and counselors. In these ways, the experience of both groups would be enriched.

24

Fees

FEES ARE A DIFFICULT SUBJECT and really outside the scope of this book if the reader is looking for actual pricing suggestions. Inflation, not to mention discretion, prohibits my giving actual figures for dog owner counseling. I will offer some guidelines.

The best advice is to check around in your area to see what other trainers and specialists are asking for their services. Obviously, a beginning counselor may not feel that he or she can ask the same fee requested by a veterinarian who treats problem behavior. Some beginning trainers effectively squelch their chances at success in this field by asking exorbitant fees. Other more experienced counselors, especially those who have published or lectured widely, price themselves out of the market—unless they treat only the canine companions of the jet set—hoping their "fame" will secure the fee.

Obviously, this kind of work should not be done for free, unless one is working in cooperation with a humane organization or a veterinarian in a concerted effort to save canine lives regardless of the cost. And, incidentally, every counselor should at least offer his or her services to humane officials—it might save a dog from being euthanized needlessly. No client, however, should get off scot-free, unless real hardship is the case. Clients simply do not value or appreciate services they do not pay for. In a materialistic society this is a sad reality. So, it is wise to ask for a fee that will neither break the bank nor delude the client into thinking you like this work so much you just need taxi fare or 25¢ to keep the coffee pot full.

Two trainers in Northern New Jersey ask at least $40 for the initial interview and then drop the fee substantially as training progresses. They explain, "The high initial cost urges the client to be serious about training, and the casual attitude that mars attempts by students in large 15-25 dollar park type obedience courses, and thus hinders their progress and the progress of others in the class, quickly evaporates when the client is faced with shelling out this large fee for the initial interview. When this client walks in, he or she is *really* ready to listen, to learn, and to work toward a betterment of their relationship with the dog."

This is one approach. On the other hand, many clients may be scared off by a high initial fee, wondering what they are going to "get" in return for their investment. Then too, the "what-am-I-going-to-get-out-of-this" mentality is a dangerous and hindering mentality in many trainer/client relationships and at least it is reduced with this method—the client shells out a higher fee and essentially agrees to take a risk. Risk taking liberates and frees and *this* element is essential in the relationship between you and your clients—they must trust you.

Most counselors, however, will stick to a middle figure for the initial interview, but we have found trainers who are naive or just reluctant to ask high fees, and even *any* fee for their services. "After all, I enjoy this type of work," said one trainer. "Why should I ask someone to pay through the nose for work I enjoy?" There is a point here, but your sheer enjoyment will not pay the oil bill. Nor will it give you any real sense of accomplishment or security. The only result of non-fee charging or low-fee charging is requests for more "freebies." Word of free services spreads quickly and the number of dog owners who need help is seemingly limitless. In fact, every time a puppy is born there is a potential client that you could, out of your intense humanitarian concern, service for free. All this ignores the possible harmful effects that free services have on non-paying clients. A loss of pride, integrity, sense of caring for one's dog can be the result.

A word here about the phone: *never* give advice over the phone unless you are being paid for it. Callers will often attempt to get you to diagnose problem behavior and give instant solutions over the phone. Many trainers will cooperate, most veterinarians will not— and with good reason. As soon as you help one person, for free, over the phone, they will tell their friends, who will tell *their* friends. It mushrooms. Indicate clearly that you cannot be of any help over the phone. Most clients will understand if you simply say, "I'm sorry,

Because you work with dogs does not mean that you are available twenty-four hours a day to answer any pet question that comes into someone's mind.

I've never met you or your dog, and I'm sure you understand that I can't be of any help over the phone." Then, redirect the client to making an appointment with you. The same holds for free advice solicited at cocktail parties, at the supermarket and even at family affairs. Because you work with dogs does not mean that you are available twenty-four hours a day to answer any pet question that comes into someone's mind. I guess I stress not doing "freebies" so strongly because I have seen the rust-out and burn-out that accompanies free advice-giving. Wendy Volhard once remarked, "The average length of time for people in dogs seems to be five years—then they burn out—because they don't know how to structure their time." Wise perception—and part of structuring your time is learning to say NO, loud and clear.

Fees should be quoted accurately over the phone, in advance. They should not be revealed, upped or lowered later. Absolute ethicality is called for in the matter of fees, careful records should be kept, sound business practices followed and a detailed record of the fees given to the client. Dog owner counseling is not a "Mom and Pop" type of operation where one can nonchalantly request a dollar here and a dollar there.

In line with this, we should note that advertisements by trainers should quote fees accurately, and should be displayed in an ethical, attractive manner. Trainers who run tacky ads trumpeting the number of dogs trained—a kind of McDonald's approach: one billion sold here!—do neither themselves nor other trainers any favors. Usually half the dogs were trained by assistants or by the owners themselves anyway. Guard dog and attack dog firms that use emotional language (Don't live in fear!) and play on the paranoia of the elderly in their ads should cease and desist, but probably won't. Ultimately, such advertising gives all trainers a bad name, and a "money-grabbing" image.

Finally, counselors should acquaint themselves with the humane movement in their locality and offer to be of help wherever they can, as our skills often save animal lives and relieve human anguish. The selfish trainer, as with the selfish professional in any field, simply deprives himself or herself of avenues for charity, personal growth and satisfaction, if making a buck, regardless of the consequences, is the main goal. Generosity and charity toward animals in need, especially those cared for in shelters, should mark our profession, since we have been graced to work with beings whose altruism, loyalty and willingness to serve should affect our own lives.

25
Exposing the
Concept

ONE PROBLEM with dog owner counseling is that the public is not well enough acquainted with it. The public consciousness of how to get dogs trained still centers on the park type obedience course or on how-to manuals. When the typical dog owner hears about counseling he or she may conjure up an image of a dog on a Freudian couch, with the counselor taking notes. Or perhaps the positions are reversed and the dog takes notes as the counselor spills out his guts. The media then gets into the act with these admittedly funny images and centers its coverage along the lines of tongue in cheek comedy. None of this really helps our field.

Recently, however, a mini-breakthrough of sorts happened when NBC's *Monitor* news program did an extended twenty minute feature on Mr. Ray McSoley, a counselor who works out of Angell Memorial Hospital in Boston and also does private work with dogs and cats. It was a sensitive piece that carefully detailed Mr. McSoley's approach to many behavior problems and showed him actually working with problem dogs and cats, and interviewing owners. The comedy aspect was held to an absolute minimum and by the time the piece was completed, one had a real understanding of both what happens in dog owner counseling and how it differs from usual training. Mr. McSoley handled himself exceptionally well, patiently explaining his techniques and elevating the whole concept of dog owner counseling in the public mind. *Monitor* and NBC should also be commended.

Almost every dog owner counselor must agree to some publicity, and some actively seek it. While it is not always possible to control what an article, radio piece or television segment will depict, you can attempt to discuss guidelines with the reporter or interviewer before the writing or taping begins.

In order to help yourself to obtain the best possible publicity and in order to help the overall field of dog owner counseling, here are some tips:

1) Do not purvey yourself as a "dog psychologist" unless you will have ample opportunity to describe your work and unless you have the appropriate degrees. The public often misunderstands this phrase and the inappropriate visions described above come immediately to mind.

2) Do not allow your work to be portrayed as pure comedy.

3) Emphasize (in what you say and do) sensitivity, humane concern and stewardship, love for dogs *and* people.

4) Do not attempt to hand out quickie solutions to pet problems via the press. Radio shows with call-in questions have to be answered very carefully—and don't hesitate to reply that the problem cannot be handled on the air and demands counseling and training.

If you may not have control over what the media says about your work, you certainly have complete control over what you say about your work in your own literature and in advertising. When I was setting up *Patience of Job: Training for Dogs and People,* one of the first studies I made was of the dog training ads in the Manhattan yellow pages. It was a revealing exercise. Of the forty plus ads, about thirty seemed to stress effectiveness, control, and reliability. Several blatantly played on the paranoia of the urban dweller and offered guard dogs, and a few stressed patience, affection, humane treatment and loving care. Many seemed more like ads offering a *product* than a *service* and in some ads, if the words "dog training" were taken out and "car washing" substituted, the telephone company could still run the ad unchanged.

Then there was the classic push to be first in the listings—"Academy of Dog Training," "Advanced Dog Training," and even "ABC Dog School!" The best ads simply stated the name of the organization, a phone number, address and a few words encouraging the dog owner to call—and promised nothing. They were refreshing in their honesty and directness. Portray yourself in advertising and in the media as the professional you are.

26

Read All About It: Which Dog Books Are Best?

IF YOU'RE LIKE MOST PEOPLE involved in dogs, you have limited time for reading, since you spend so much time with animals. Perhaps some advice on which dog books are best would be of help to you. I had to do an incredible amount of reading in my early years in dogs, because as a member of a monastery, I was not allowed to attend seminars or clinics due to the rules of the community. Later, I was able to attract most of the teachers I admired to the monastery for private seminars, but in the beginning, I had to rely primarily on reading to gain technical knowledge.

My self-study course included all of the standard breeding and training texts. And I was able to glean an extraordinary amount of information from the other brothers. In the early days the reading was divided up amongst the monks so that one monk read everything he could about veterinary medicine, another read up on pedigrees and I covered behavior and training. Then, we would get together and pool our knowledge. This communal learning approach greatly accelerated the learning process. Unfortunately, most people have not had the opportunity to live in a community where everyone is intent on reading similar material and sharing what they've learned. Ideally, breed and obedience clubs should operate this way, but some members are secretive and guarded about their hard-won knowledge and will not share with others. Nevertheless, many clubs now maintain good libraries and you can find a helpful list of books there.

One of the best books I've found for children who are anticipating a new dog is *Some Swell Pup,* by Matthew Margolis, and illustrated by the extremely popular and talented artist Maurice Sendack (Farrar, Straus and Giroux, New York, 1976). This book spells out the whole process of getting and keeping a puppy, especially some of the responsibilities involved. The colorful drawings will add to the delight of any child and will definitely aid the whole family's enjoyment of the dog. And this is by no means the only book for children, but I'll let someone more knowledgeable in children's literature cover this topic.

For adults, the field is so wide open it's very difficult to select what's good. The back of every book will say something to the effect that this is the *newest* method for training dogs. Some will tell you this is the *only* method for training dogs. Others will come right out and tell you that unless you get this book you will never understand your dog and he will probably hate you (if he doesn't already). A lot of the titles play on two aspects: you don't understand your dog and you sure would like to, wouldn't you? and, your dog is supposed to be your friend and he probably isn't and it's your fault. Thus, the plethora of "palsy" titles: *Your Dog, Your Pal, My Friend, Fido,* even *How to Be Your Dog's Best Friend* (in case he isn't his own).

As a consequence, after visiting a bookstore and buying one of these tracts, most dog owners go home to read it burdened with guilt. Many probably hide from the dog while reading it!

Don't let such titles get you down—half of them are creations from publishers' staff meetings. A flaky title doesn't necessarily mean that the book has nothing to say to you. However, do avoid any books that claim miracle methods that involve absolutely no disciplining of the dog. These books will parade themselves as "humane" answers to other "dog-beating" books. The gullible public (after all, no one wants to hit a dog) snatches up such books, only to find that within, the author suggests no *physical* discipline methods, but plenty of useless ones—expensive "sound-therapy" devices (sometimes a coupon is attached in the rear of the book), rattling pennies in a can (try to stop a dog fight using that technique) or even using "thought waves" to "will" the dog back into obedience.

The fact is, discipline is an essential part of the dog/owner covenant, and any owner who refuses to dish it out (when truly necessary) is just asking for trouble. Similarily, any book on dogs that just avoids the topic of discipline or correction does the reading public a disservice. Avoid such books.

Now that you have your ground rules, you go out book hunting. Look immediately for Dr. Michael Fox's *Understanding Your Dog* (Coward, McCann and Geoghegan, 1972). Dr. Fox is well known to the American public through his "Tonight Show" appearances and his many other books. This, one of his first popular publishing efforts, has been very successful for him and can be found in hardback or paperback in any bookstore or library. It is based on solid scientific research and gives you a look at your dog's brain and emotions. Fox even shows inklings in this book of his later mystical and religious leanings and he certainly lets you know that owning a dog is a spiritual and philosophical experience, one that is loaded with responsibilities. I've heard of people who, after reading just Dr. Fox's book, decided *not* to get a dog—having realized the tremendous bargain it entails between animal and man. Certainly that's one of the highest compliments that can be paid any book on dogs.

Look again for a second *Understanding Your Dog,* not by Dr. Fox but by Eberhard Trumler, with a foreword by Konrad Lorenz (Faber and Faber, Queen Square, London). Originally published as *Your Dog and You* and then allowed to go out of print, this English effort is on a par with Fox's book and unfortunately now sports the same title. Trumler, a Lorenz disciple, carefully charts out the primitive nature of the dog, the concept of imprinting, early training, and the stages of puberty and maturity. Illustrations of wolves, coyotes and dogs abound. It's an excellent overview, preferably read pre-dog ownership.

Two more British books need mention immediately as superlative. Both are by John Holmes, a training enthusiast and, obviously, dog lover. *The Family Dog* (1957) and *The Farmer's Dog* (1960, both Popular Dogs Publishing, Great Britain) are two well rounded tracts aimed at the family who has a house pet. Neither emphasize competition training or show ring training. Ironically, I've found *The Farmer's Dog* to be of most help to dog owners in cities and suburbia. Both contain reams of insight and knowledge gleaned over many hard years of training dogs for show, competition and herding trials. Interestingly, both are dedicated to the dogs themselves, not to any human interloper. The writing style is early James Herriot, and delightful.

Kinship with All Life and *The Language of Silence* (Harper and Row) are only partially about dogs, but they are to be highly suggested for what they say about animals and nature in general. The theme of both books by J. Allen Boone, an ex-Hollywood producer of animal films, is *listening.* This necessarily involves some amount of silence on the part of the human if the dog is to be allowed to say anything. In chapter after subtle chapter, Boone is telling us, in essence, to shut up. Any professional who works with animals will tell you that's just excellent advice. The section on the Hollywood dog, Strongheart, in *Kinship with All Life,* is a classic. Boone describes going out into the desert to meet Mohave Dan, an old hermit who has the "secret" to communicating with animals. The hermit's advice:

> There's facts about dogs, and there's opinions about them. The dogs have the facts, and the humans have the opinions. If you want facts about a dog, always get them straight from the dog.

That's about as close to a zen koan as you'll come in dog literature, and if there is only one book you read suggested in this capter, let it be *Kinship with All Life.* But don't think that you won't be hooked enough to procur *The Language of Silence* too, for it is more of the same top-quality writing and advice.

Another book, *Dog Problems,* by Carol Lea Benjamin (Doubleday, 1981) also makes my list. The blunt title might steer puppy owners away from the book, but they are the people who should own it and read it *before* the onset of problems. Benjamin's theory is sound: anticipate problems with your dog, and if you already have them, don't remain passive about them. This is not good for the dog, since it is looking to you for leadership. If you can't or won't provide the needed leadership, the dog is going to attempt to lead *you* and then you will really be in a mess. Practically every problem is handled—chewing, digging, aggression, nervousness, shyness, carsickness, you name it, it's here. But the book is only 180 pages long. Why, if she's covering so many problems? Because her basic approach is a thread that weaves itself throughout the book and places the responsibility squarely on the owner. It is the thread of

150

stewardship and *leadership,* two concepts that have ramifications not just in dog studies but in many areas of the ecological fields. All of the best dog books, you will notice, stress these two concepts, whether the matter at hand is correcting the dog for chewing a slipper, or simply gazing at your dog as he stands nobly with a mountain vista as his backdrop. In the best dog books, you'll always feel a sense of appreciation for the mystery that dogs are—a sense of gratitude for the great gift they are to us, and a corresponding desire to care for them and lead them on to greater heights. Even if a problem is being discussed, this will come through, as it does in Carol Benjamin's book. She uses a Chinese proverb to open the book, and it sums up her approach to dogs: "Never use a hatchet to remove a fly from the forehead of a friend."

A standardized, but excellent care and training book is *The Good Dog Book,* by Mordecai Siegal (Macmillan, 1977). All of the standard information is here and more. There are chapters on weight watching for your dog, disasters, and old age. Here's another interesting standard by which to judge a dog book: does the author ever address the problems of the older dog and the problem of what to do when a dog dies? Siegal does, devoting a whole chapter to it. If an author mentions this area and gives some treatment to the topic, it probably reveals that he or she has seen dog life from start to finish. Breeders, for instance, who see dog life as it begins and as it ends, often write in this vein. It's a healthy approach, for it sees canine life in terms of an overall process, a continuum.

Human adults got all excited a few years back about a book called *Passages,* which charted out life stages. Everyone began figuring out which stage they were in and what kind of problems they should be having. Dogs, too, go through stages, and at a very rapid pace. Adolescence, for instance, in dogs, takes about a year or two. Try foisting a two year adolescence, with its accompanying mental and physical growth pains, on any human teenager and you'll see a rebellion that will make James Dean seem saintly. Yet, dogs pass through this hectic stage in a flash, often with little understanding from their keepers. Good dog books will recognize this concept of life stages. You'll be able to tell if they do by skimming the chapter headings.

Nor should the eminent Konrad Lorenz be forgotten in this overview. His *Man Meets Dog* (Penguin paperback) is a classic

151

with dog people and nature lovers, and rightfully so. Although he propounds an erroneous hypothesis: that the bulk of domestic dogs are descended from the golden Jackal, *Canis aureus* (a theory he later recanted in his foreword to *The Wild Canids*), Lorenz is on solid turf in most of his observations. His early feelings, back in the 1950's, that dogs could experience emotions, such as remorse or envy, later set the tone for discoveries by other observers and helped shape training techniques in later decades.

Behavior Problems in Dogs, by William E. Campbell, another excellent book stuck with a starchy title, had a great effect on dog trainers, veterinarians and breeders when it was first published in 1975 (American Veterinary Publictions, Santa Barbara, CA). It was the first book to discuss at length the concept of dog owner counseling—that a trainer or a veterinarian could, *should* actually sit down with a client and interview them concerning the health and behavior of the pet in order to get at the bottom of the pet's difficulties.

While it sounds like a terribly obvious approach, the fact is, most dogs in America and Europe are still herded into dog obedience classes, trained en masse in courses usually stretching over 8-10 weeks, using techniques developed in Germany before World War I when dogs had to be trained in a hurry to get them positioned for battle. Consequently, these field techniques rarely if ever take into consideration the problems and needs of the domestic dog owner and the peculiar problems of particular breeds. Campbell does, and the way to get to the bottom of these problems, he says, is to sit down and make a study of the dog in much the same way as a psychiatrist would interview a patient. Since the dog can't talk, the human has to provide some of the information. But here's the catch—the humans only give part of the facts—they lie, they underplay, they avoid talking about the dog's problems, even as they seek help in solving them.

Campbell's contribution lies in the fact that he took the whole dog training and care game a little more seriously than most of his contemporaries. He has absolutely no patience with stop-gap measures or with folklore and training myths. He goes right to the heart of the dog's needs and the client's needs. Again, that sense of appreciation for the dogs, even if crudely offset by an intolerance of their human masters, comes through. Stylistically—he's devilish.

The chapter "Problem Owners and Characteristics" completely turns the tables around from the usual approach found in canine books. Usually it's the *dogs* that are being categorized and then described so that their owners can "understand" them better. Book after book will list "canine types" such as "the nervous dog," "the biter," "the hood," "the brat," "the lethargic dog," "the chewer" and on and on—always putting the onus for bad behavior squarely on the dog. As if the *dog* deliberately thwarted its own development! A cheap ploy, when you think about it, and when you know the real facts—although such categorizations undoubtedly make dog owners feel better.

Campbell, meanwhile takes the owners to task using the typology we listed early in this book. He characterizes *them.* And, with his long list of owner-types, hardly anyone escapes. It was a wonderful idea and perhaps partially an attack.

Anyone involved in dog owner counseling has to read *Behavior Problems in Dogs*—simply has to. It is the standard text and will remain so for some time. I would suggest it to your clients, too, as it will give them invaluable information and help them to see that dog owner counseling is a unique and growing field. While the book is not really addressed to the lay person, anyone can read it easily, and should—it is a book for every counselor, veterinarian, trainer—and all students of the *Canid* family.

Two excellent books on the more technical aspects of training are *How to Be Your Dog's Best Friend* (Little, Brown, 1978) which I have already praised, and *Training Your Dog, The Step by Step Manual,* by Joachim Volhard and Gail Tamases Fisher. First, a few more words on the monks' book. Besides the technical sections, there are sections on praise, discipline, massage for dogs, silence and the dog, where the dog should sleep in the evening and a host of other concerns. It is really a life manual for both dog and owner. Again, I highly recommend it.

Training Your Dog (Howell Book House, 1983) grew partially out of the enormously popular seminars taught by the husband and wife team, Jack and Wendy Volhard. You would be hard-pressed to find a tighter, more highly organized and articulate seminar in the dog fancy today, and the resulting book has the same traits. An amazing amount of technical skill is communicated through the text and photographs, and the cartoons which I mentioned earlier, are priceless. The opening section on "The Mind of the Dog" is valuable because so few training books discuss this all-important matter. A final section on behavior problems is one of the best reasoned short essays on the general area I've read. There is a good bibliography and the index is helpful. The training progressions throughout couldn't be more clear, and you will find this a useful guide for teacher or student. The book has an excellent sense of humor, and the use of the name "Konrad" throughout rather than just "the dog" is charming and comical in and of itself.

Writing about animal communication demands extraordinary writing skills—and Emily Hahn, an ex-English teacher and animal lover, has such skills in abundance. Back in 1978 she published *Look Who's Talking* (Thomas Crowell, New York), a book about the communicative skills of animals. She contacted leading scientists actively working with apes, wolves and dogs, as well as "non-experts"—trainers, breeders and handlers. The latter group often proved to be more "expert" and perceptive in their observations than the real experts. This is an irony those of us in the dog fancy are well acquainted with. For instance, veterinarians are often asked for advice on dog behavior problems, even though most will admit that they have little or no knowledge in the area, other than knowing the standard folklore that surrounds the subject. The ordinary breeder or trainer, meanwhile, might know exactly what to do about a biting or chewing problem.

Hahn's style is crisp and enjoyable. Many times she simply lets her subjects talk—as she does in the chapter on Dr. Michael Fox, whom she visited at Washington University in St. Louis around the same time I did. In this sterling chapter, Hahn so submerges herself in order to let her subject talk, that you feel you are in the room talking to Dr. Fox. If you have a dog, cat or a bowl of goldfish, you'll gain from reading this book, and when you're done, you'll know more about yourself.

If you are working in the area of counseling dog owners, you will want to be acquainted with basic counseling texts. The forementioned books by Virginia Satir are essential and will help to highlight the points in this book. I would also suggest a working knowledge of the works of Abraham Maslow. The books by Eugene Kennedy on counseling are also helpful. When you read such books you will have to apply what you are reading to the peculiar nature of

154

your own profession, because, up until the time of this book, there was no text for dog owner counselors. So, we have to draw from other sources.

If you are shy or have difficulty talking with others you will find counseling dog owners a trial, no matter how much you love dogs. One book I have found helpful is *How to Talk to Practically Anyone About Practically Anything,* by Barbara Walters. She, too, discusses personality types and how to deal with them (Pocket Books, 1970).

For a better understanding of the nature of criticism, you might try *Nobody's Perfect* (Stratford Press, 1982) by Dr. Hendrie Weisinger and Norman M. Lobenz. This useful guide may make it easier for you to lower the axe on a dog owner who is bungling his or her relationship with a dog.

That's my rundown on the books that have helped me in my work and I hope will help you in yours. Canine studies is a new and evolving field, especially in the area of training technique, behavior problems, socialization techniques, nutrition and human/dog interaction in general. We're sure to see many more excellent books come from the pens of authors like Carol Benjamin, Emily Hahn, Michael Fox, John Holmes, Mordecai Siegal and William Campbell, all of whom are actively writing on the two topics that fascinate them the most: dogs and people.

27

A Final Word

It should be clear then, that the whole point of dog owner counseling is that the relationship between man and dog is one that entails a *covenant*. This covenant is the same whether it be between a man and dog or between mankind as a whole and creation. There are responsibilities on both sides. It is a covenant of *stewardship,* first and foremost, for man agrees to care for creation, to care for the dog. Part of this care is humane training—and part of training is counseling.

The relationship between an owner and dog is *not* just an agreement between master and slave, and in fact, I dislike the term "owner" and have used it only because the alternatives are few. The dog is not a "product" that the human uses, not a commodity to be squandered. The dog is a living being who looks to us for guidance and support.

Behind many efforts in animal training is simply a utilitarian motive—to get the animal to do something, or else. But the best ethos for training is to elevate the animal to a new level. As J. Allen Boone once remarked in *Kinship with All Life,* "There is a difference between *training* an animal and *educating* one. Trained animals are relatively easy to turn out. All that is required is a book of instructions, a certain amount of bluff and bluster, something to use for threatening and punishing purposes, and of course the animal. Educating an animal, on the other hand, demands keen intelligence, integrity, imagination, and the gentle touch, mentally, vocally and physically." Realizing this opens us up to the fact that all of our relationships with animals and nature revolve around our ability to give responsible stewardship.

My hope is that in the future dog owner counseling will be

156

available to many more who love dogs than it is today. Through it, I believe we will save many dog owners and dogs countless hours of frustration and anguish. For many dogs, it may literally save their lives. The greatest joy in life is to help someone—or to help them to help someone they love—including their dog.

It is a covenant of stewardship.

INDEX